Invest in Fear

Invest in Fear
How to profit from financial storms with volatility

Ramin Charles Nakisa

Chesham Bois Publishing

Chesham Bois Publishing

21 Chestnut Close, Amersham, HP6 6EQ

First published in 2014 by Chesham Bois Publishing

Printed and bound in Great Britain by Lightning Source UK Ltd.

Typeset using L$_Y$X

Calculations in R, graphs in ggplot2

British Library Cataloguing in Publication Data. A catalogue record for this book is available from the British Library.

Rev : 2241

ISBN 978-0-9566635-1-1

To my family

Acknowledgements

I would like to thank my family for listening to my tirades about volatility, Philip French for his editing skills and helpful comments, Frank Velling for his insightful comments on crisis turning points, Youssef Intabli at Bloomberg who provided invaluable help and support, Sinan Kömür for feeding me at the Hard Wok Café in the Liverpool Street Arcade, and my fellow commuters on the Metropolitan line from Amersham to the City who were jostled while this book was being written.

Contents

1 What is volatility?

"To deal with black swans, we instead need things that gain from volatility, variability, stress and disorder."

Nassim Nicholas Taleb

The purpose of this book is to explain how to invest in something that you can't touch or feel. It is also a thing that most people do not understand or even fear because they think it is too complex. Some people equate it with fear itself. This investment is volatility. The best foil to fear is understanding, and the information contained here will explain volatility in simple terms. My aim is to convince you that volatility should be part of your diversified investment portfolio alongside shares and bonds at least some of the time. If after reading this book you feel you still don't understand volatility, unlikely as that may be, then don't invest in it. I recommend spending a little time to get to grips with the ideas presented here, because this will open up a whole new asset class that has only become available to the broader market quite recently.

There are now a wide range of volatility products that trade just like shares, or as *exchange traded products* (ETP). This means that you just look up the ticker "VXX" on your broker's web site, click on buy and you become a volatility investor. No, wait, don't click on "buy" yet! Read this book first so you know what you're doing. The names of volatility exchange traded products are notoriously difficult. They are identified via a confusing mixture of the letters "X", "V" and "Z". If you get confused about the difference between VIX, XVZ, VXX, and VXZ then there is an appendix at the back of the book called the "Volatility Glossary" (see Chapter 5) that describes each product briefly. Place a marker there for quick reference. The structure of the book is as follows:

Chapter 1: What is volatility? Introduces the concept of volatility using Google's share price as an example. Volatility surges during crises so we look at these "tail events" over the last 140 years to get a feel for how often crises occurred in the past. Volatility is measured for US stocks using an index called VIX, and we introduce VIX and other volatility indices. We finish with an explanation of volatility term structure and the difference between implied and realized volatility.

Chapter 2: A brief history of volatility What news items drive volatility higher and lower? This brief pictorial history answers this question and is split into four sections: the period from 1950 to 1990 before there were any volatility indices, then from the birth of VIX in 1990 to just before the Credit Crisis in 2007, then detailed sections on the Credit Crisis and European sovereign debt crisis. Finally there is a section on crisis keywords which shows how you might be able to use the frequency of search terms on Google to gauge the level of volatility for the *crisis du jour*.

Chapter 3: How to invest in volatility Explores the large and growing family of exchange traded products that are linked to volatility, explaining what exchange traded products are, their drawbacks and risks, the idea of roll cost and how it affects different volatility products. This chapter also explains short volatility, levered volatility and dynamic volatility exchange traded products.

Chapter 4: Volatility trading strategies Presents three simple trading strategies which have worked profitably in the past. By counting the number of days VIX is above a threshold the strategies provide a guide to help you time your trades. These are intended as examples to help you develop your own VIX trading strategies suited to your own investment style and appetite for risk.

Chapter 5: The Future The last decade contains two global financial crises. If, like me, you believe these next decade will not contain another major global crisis what would the best portfolio look like and how would this affect the trading strategies in Chapter 4?

There are some concepts that you can't skip, such as VIX term structure and roll cost, which are fundamental for volatility investment. If you understand these concepts you will be much more likely to invest profitably in volatility. Those who understand volatility already can probably jump to Chapter 4 on "How to invest in volatility", perhaps stopping to muse at the lessons learned in the "Brief History of Volatility". For those who aren't familiar with volatility I've provided a gentle introduction in these first two chapters with no mathematics at all.

Hedging or investing?

It is possible to gamble with volatility, as with any other financial instrument. By gamble I mean placing a huge proportion of your capital into a volatility instrument in the hope it will gain in value. This is not a good idea because concentrating all your capital in one investment is extremely risky. I will focus here on volatility as an *investment*. That means we will look at volatility as part of a well-balanced portfolio of stocks and shares. In this regard investment is rather like the food that you eat. Ice cream is tasty, but you would soon become ill on a diet of ice cream alone. The goal is to achieve a well-balanced diet of investments, and volatility should be thought of as a nutritional addition to your investment menu. Volatility can improve your returns but you have to be aware of its rather unique characteristics to use it to its full potential.

The first surprising thing is that if you hold a long-term position in volatility you will almost certainly lose money. This is the exact opposite of shares or bonds where holding a position in a share or bond index for several decades will almost certainly make money. To understand why this is the case a good analogy is the purchase of life insurance. As an individual you buy life insurance because a single, catastrophic tail event resulting in the loss of your life is a risk you cannot afford to take when you have dependents. You will probably lose out on this insurance contract because you will pay your insurance premium for all of your adult life, but losing out is actually what you want. Few people think along the following lines: "That's great! I'm going to die, then I can claim on my life insurance!". Sellers of life insurance make a profit because, on average, the premium they receive more than compensates them for the payouts they make. Individually you will probably lose out, but you are willing to pay the insurance premium because your family depends on you financially. Similarly, if you buy insurance against stock market crashes all the time then over the long term you will lose out, but on the rare occasions when the market crashes you will be glad of the protection.

The flip side of the long-term fall of volatility positions is that you can reverse the sign. Instead of buying volatility, which is like buying insurance, you can sell volatility. Instead of being *long* volatility you will be *short* volatility. A long volatility position will lose money in the long-run but during a stock market crash will harvest significant gains. A short volatility position will make money in the long-run but is very risky because during a crisis it will make significant losses. We will return to these ideas in much more detail in Chapter 3 on "How to invest in volatility" which shows how to go long or short volatility with exchange traded products.

Typically people think of volatility in two ways: hedging and investing. In practice the difference is not so clear-cut because some volatility products are designed to be long-term investments (see the section "Reducing roll cost" in Chapter 3). These two approaches to volatility can be summarized as follows:

Hedging Investors can buy volatility as a way of *hedging*. The idea of hedging, which is buying assets to reduce your portfolio's risk, is something you are probably familiar with, in the phrase "hedging your bets". The riskiest part of your portfolio will almost certainly be your shares. If you want to reduce the risk of losing money on your shares you can buy something that goes up in value when shares fall in value. The effect is to dampen the overall volatility of your portfolio, and also the risk of extreme losses. Of course nothing comes for free, and you have to pay for this hedge. Volatility pays out during market shocks and crises, but the simple fact is that crises are rare. All the time that you own a volatility product you will be paying your insurance premium and most of the time this will lose money.

Investing Investors can buy volatility when they think it will rise and sell volatility when they think it will fall. This is treating volatility just like any other asset class such as a share or a bond: buy low, sell high. A side effect of buying volatility for an equity investor is that it acts as a hedge for their stocks.

Timing your purchase and sale, which is important for any investment, is particularly important for volatility. Volatility is rather like a sleeping dragon. Most of the time it lies asleep on its hoard of treasure. However if there is a market shock the dragon wakes. The trick is knowing what kind of headlines wake the dragon. For example, with the benefit of hindsight there were many signals that the Credit Crisis was about to explode. At the time however it was hard to pick out the signs amidst the euphoria of rising house prices and rising share prices. Later in the book (in Chapter 4) we will see some trading strategies that use simple signals to suggest when you should buy and when you should sell volatility.

How volatile is Google?

A good way to begin is to define exactly what we mean by volatility for a stock we all know. If you invest in shares you know that the price of shares goes up and down on a daily basis. Each share has a pattern of movements, almost like a fingerprint, that define its daily price changes. Some shares fluctuate a lot more than others. We can characterize these daily movements very simply by looking at the average daily percentage move. For example, Figure 1.1 shows the share price and daily returns of Google over a two week period.

During this two week period we see three days of price falls and seven days of price gains. This was a quiet period because a typical daily move for a share, either up or down, was around 1% to 2%. The typical daily move, or *volatility* of Google from 2004 to 2013 is around 2.1% but during this quiet week it was just 1%. Just as interest rates are standardized and quoted as annualized rates, volatility is annualized too, and here we can use a trader's trick. To convert daily volatility to annualized volatility we just multiply by sixteen.[1] The calculation of volatility is simple, for example you can use the STDEV function in Excel. In case you are interested this is how it works, and the numbers are shown in Figure 1.1 in case you wanted try the five stage calculation yourself:

- **Average return**: calculate the average return (+0.23% during these two weeks in 2013 for Google).

- **Throw away the sign**: calculate the square of the difference between the average return and each daily return. All the squared deviations from the mean return will be zero or positive.

- **Daily variance**: sum the squared deviations from the average and divide by the number of returns minus one.

- **Daily volatility**: take the square root of the daily variance to get daily volatility.

- **Annualized volatility**: multiply daily volatility by sixteen to get the annualized volatility. More accurately we annualize the daily volatility by multiplying by the square root of the 252 trading days in a year. The square root of 252 is 15.87, a little bit less than 16.

During this quiet two week period daily volatility of 1% equates to an annualized volatility just 15.6%. Over a much longer period from 2004 to 2013 Google's daily volatility of 2% equates to an annualized volatility of 32%.

---

[1] Volatility scales as the square root of time, and as there are about 252 trading days in a year to convert one day volatility to one year volatility we scale up by $\sqrt{252}$ which is roughly 16.

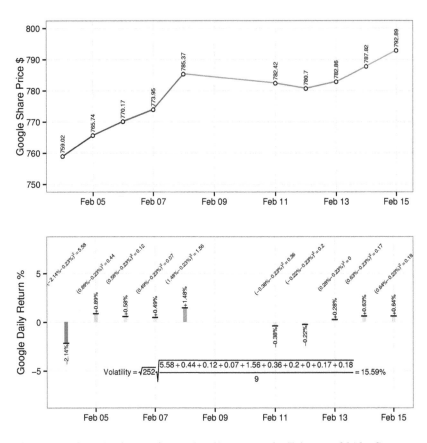

Figure 1.1: Google share price and daily returns in February 2013. Source: Bloomberg.

Shares of a large and successful company such as Google would typically have an annual volatility of around 30% under normal market conditions.

Because volatility defines a typical daily return we can then judge whether a daily return is not typical. Volatility can be thought of as a "surprise yardstick". A typical daily move of 2% means a typical annual move of 32%. In other words it is totally unsurprising for a stock to either gain or lose 30% in one year or to gain or lose 2% in a day. However a daily move of 4% is surprising and a daily move of 6% is very surprising indeed.

Now have a look at two weeks of Google returns just at the turning point of the Credit Crisis in March 2009, a time of great volatility and large daily returns for all stocks in Figure 1.2. Instead of 1% or 2% moves we are now seeing several daily moves, both rises and falls, of 5% or more. Volatility in March 2009 is obviously much higher than the previous example in February 2013 (daily volatility was 3.4%, annualized this is 54%). In fact at this time volatility was high for almost all stocks, bonds, currencies and commodities.

An important aspect of volatility is that it does not care whether the share price moves up or down. The actual calculation of volatility squares each daily move before adding up the values and taking the average. Squaring a number throws away the sign such that negative becomes positive and positive stays positive. If volatility is a measure of risk ignoring the sign of returns may seem strange because we are very happy about a move upward in a share but very unhappy about a downward move. Why count the upward move too if this isn't really a "risk"? The reason is rather surprising. If you put all the daily movements of a stock into two buckets, an up bucket and a down bucket and then count the number of days in each bucket they will be roughly equal. If you calculate the average size of an up-move and a down-move the numbers are also roughly equal. In other words the average down move is about the same size as the average up move.

Our bucket analysis will lead us to a staggering revelation: *buying an asset means buying a return distribution*. The word "distribution" may sound scary, but all that it means is the pattern of daily stock price movements, which is like the stock's fingerprint. A volatility investor should know and understand the *probability distribution* of the stock they are trading. A stock investor is interested in the direction in which a stock price moves, either up or down. In contrast, a volatility investor is only interested in the size of the price moves, not their direction. If the volatility investor has bought volatility they want big daily moves of the share price either up or down. If they have sold volatility they want small daily moves either up or down.

To deepen our understanding of return distributions we need to make our

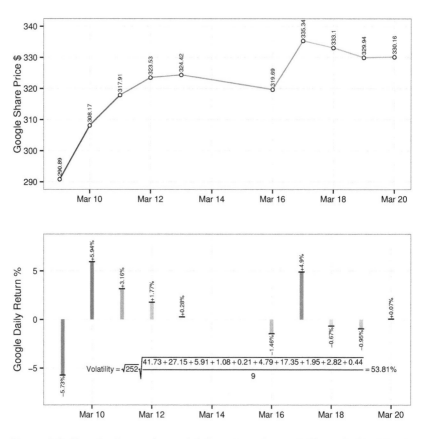

Figure 1.2: Google share price and daily returns in a volatile period in March 2009. Source: Bloomberg.

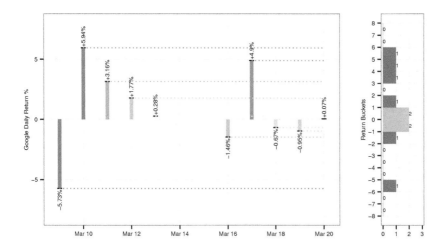

Figure 1.3: Volatile week for Google in March 2009 showing daily return histogram. Source: Bloomberg.

bucket analysis a little more sophisticated by introducing more buckets. From our two week history of Google's closing price we obtain ten daily returns. The buckets chop up the range of returns into intervals and we count how often returns fall into each interval or bucket. For example we could have the sixteen buckets from -8% to +8% shown in Figure 1.3. The return on March 9th was -5.73% which goes into the -5% to -6% bucket. Dotted lines show the buckets into which each of the ten daily returns fall.

This was a choppy two weeks with some very large positive returns in the 3% to 4%, 4% to 5% and even 5% to 6% buckets and one large negative return in the -6% to -5% bucket. As we add more buckets and more returns a clearer picture emerges. We can see that the buckets with small returns (less than +2% and more than -2%) have the most counts and that large positive and negative returns (above +3% and below -3%) happen less frequently. Figure 1.4 shows the 2,248 daily Google returns between August 23rd, 2004 and July 26th, 2013 counted in 32 return buckets.

In Figure 1.5 we can see the return histogram from Figure 1.4 turned the right way up. It is striking that Google's returns are positive just 52% of the time but the positive returns were slightly larger on average (1.49%) than the negative returns (-1.37%). This slight imbalance is sufficient to increase the share price by over 700% in one decade (from $108.31 on August, 20th 2004

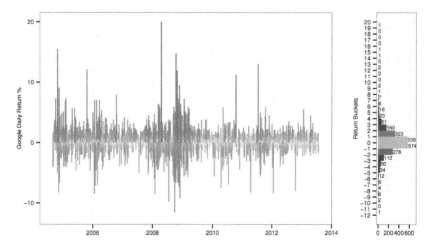

Figure 1.4: Google daily returns since 2004 showing daily return histogram.
Source: Bloomberg.

to \$885.35 on July 26th, 2013). It takes just a small shift in the balance of returns to tip our investment from profit to loss. Stock investors are betting on this imbalance being slightly positive over the long term.

Stock investors like positive returns and dislike negative returns. But what stock investors utterly abhor are very large negative returns, or *drawdowns*, because it can take a long time to recover from a price crash. Buying volatility offers a way to mitigate the effects of these drawdowns on stock portfolios because during market crashes volatility gains in value, driven higher by the large daily price movements that come with tumbling share prices. A common use of volatility is to hedge the share component of a portfolio and we will return to this idea in the "Strategy 3: Incorporating Dynamic VIX into your portfolio" section of Chapter 4 on trading strategies.

Most of the time stock prices move by a small amount, as shown in Figure 1.5. However fortunes are made and lost in the tails of the distribution which are the largest positive and negative returns. Share investors make their biggest profits with the right hand tail which is large upward movements in share prices and lose on the left hand tail. Volatility buyers make money from *both* tails and lose money in the middle of the distribution. Understanding tail events is so important that the next section deals with them in detail.

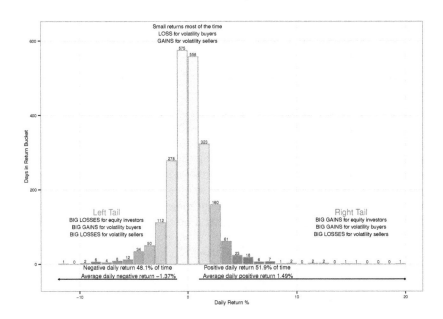

Figure 1.5: Google daily return distribution (2004 to 2013). Source: Bloomberg.

Tail events

Tail events can destroy or make a portfolio so it pays to understand their behaviour. Very large daily losses have been called "black swans" because according to some simple risk models they should never occur. [2] Optimists may
also point out that the models underestimate the occurrence of large positive
returns. We might think of these large positive returns as golden swans. Both
black swans and golden swans are created as financial markets digest new information, and in fact some people think of volatility as a measure of the rate
of flow of information in financial markets. Simplistically you might expect
that bad news makes black swans and good news makes golden swans, but as
we will see the two often clump together.

An important question we might ask is whether tail events are spaced evenly
through time or whether they occur in clusters. Or to put it another way, we
might ask whether black swans come singly or in flocks. Figure 1.6 shows
the price of the S&P 500 reconstructed by the Nobel prize-winning economist
Robert Shiller stretching back to 1870. The timeline alongside the S&P 500
picks out the golden and black swans as upward and downward arrows. The
size of the arrow reflects the size of the move that month with only moves
greater than 10% shown. A price increase of +10% or more in a month is
a golden swan and a price fall of -10% or more is a black swan. Some of
the larger crises that had a significant effect on volatility are picked out with
vertical text.

The first thing that jumps out is that there is a huge cluster of black swans
with a few golden swans around the time of the Great Depression. In 1929
there were two black swans, followed by two in 1930 and five in 1931, four in
1932, two in 1933 and one in 1934. After a three year respite there was another
recession in 1937 which sparked another two black swans. It is interesting to
see that the record golden swan of about +50% from July to August 1933
occurred in the heart of the Great Depression. We can see that golden swans
hang out with black swans. Leading up to the present day we see the 1973
oil crisis, the October 1987 crash and the bursting of the dot-com bubble in
2001. The Credit Crisis black swan in 2008 is comparable in size to those of
the Great Depression but is not as severe because there was a single, sharp
correction followed by a rebound rather than a cluster of successive disastrous

---

[2]The idea of black swans in finance was popularized by Nassim Nicholas Taleb in his book "The
Black Swan: The Impact of the Highly Improbable". European logicians often used black
swans as an example of falsifiability: if there is a belief that all swans are white then the
observation of a single black swan shows this entire system of belief is incorrect.

months.

Volatility investors thrive on tail events because extreme events and market shocks drive up the value of volatility. By throwing away the sign of share movements all swans transform into golden swans. This way the volatility investor capitalizes on all extreme share movements whether up or down. If a share price falls or rises gradually that is not particularly interesting to a volatility investor. Steady share price movements do not make volatility increase. Volatility spikes upward during crises. The bull market for volatility investors can be driven by natural disasters, financial scandals, or a positive or negative surprise in the earnings of a company. The bear market for volatility investors is a quiet market with no alarms and no surprises.

Ideally the volatility investor will buy volatility when it is cheap, during a period of market calm, and sell when it is expensive after a shock. Although this sounds simple it is not. Predicting shocks is difficult but not impossible. For example certain pivotal events are based on the calendar. For example we may know a decision will be made on a certain date, but not know the outcome of that decision. The decision might be political elections, announcement of the outcome of drug trials for a pharmaceutical company, corporate earnings announcements or legal judgments for or against a company. Anything that might shock share prices up or down will increase volatility, and the bigger the shock the better. Holding volatility exposure has a rent called roll cost which depends on the key concept of volatility term structure that we deal with in the next section.

Measuring volatility: volatility indices

In the financial press the value of major stock indices, such as the S&P 500 or the Dow Jones, are quoted all the time. Indices are useful because they provide a summary of financial markets as a single number. In one sense indices are a barometer of performance for large groups of assets. Stock indices are like a portfolio of stocks often weighted by the market capitalization of each stock. The volatility market also has indices, and the most well-known is called the VIX. The Chicago Board Options Exchange (CBOE) Volatility Index, to give its full title, measures the expected 30-day volatility of the S&P 500 share index. VIX is calculated[3] using options on stocks in the S&P 500 share index, so it is a US stock market volatility measure. There are also volatility indices

---

[3]For the exact calculation of VIX see http://www.cboe.com/micro/vix/vixwhite.pdf.

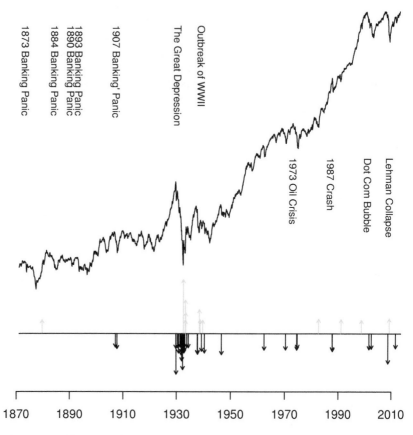

Figure 1.6: Clusters of S&P positive and negative tail events (daily gain of more than +10% or loss greater than -10%). Source: Shiller.

for the Nasdaq-100 (VXN), Dow Jones Industrial Average (VXD) and Russell 2000 (RVX) share indices but VIX is the most widely quoted and traded index.

Some people call VIX the fear index. However this is misleading, because although it is true that fear and stock market crashes drive up the value of VIX so do up-crashes. Because volatility ignores the sign of market moves an up-crash and a down-crash look the same to a pure volatility investor. So as well as being a fear index VIX is a joy index. Another way of seeing volatility is an information flow index. As new information becomes available to the market investors buy and sell more stocks and the typical daily price move of stocks increases.

In Figure 1.7 we see the S&P 500 stock index and the VIX index. There is a very clear difference between the two indices:

Drift The S&P drifts upwards and (less often) downwards over the long term but VIX does not. In theory there is no "anchor value" for the S&P 500 but VIX will *always* return to 20%. This is a very useful property if you trade VIX.

Correlation During a crisis when stock prices fall sharply VIX behaves in the opposite way and rises sharply. In other words the S&P 500 and VIX are strongly negatively correlated. Owning both is therefore less risky than owning either on their own.

European investors that do not want to buy US volatility have a local alternative. There are European volatility indices that measure the volatility of European shares. The major European volatility indices are VSTOXX, which is linked to the volatility of the EURO STOXX 50 European share index, and VDAX-NEW (usually referred to as VDAX), which is linked to the German DAX share index. Globally several other volatility indices exist (see Table 1.1) calculated in much the same way as VIX. However these indices will remain untradeable until they have active volatility futures markets.

As you can see in Figure 1.8 the three main volatility indices are very similar in their behaviour, rising and falling together almost all of the time. However there are some systematic differences. For example VIX is on average 2% lower than VDAX and 4% lower than VSTOXX. Also the source of crises affects the size of the peak in volatility. For example during the beginning of the European sovereign debt crisis in 2010 the volatility in German stocks reached a much lower peak than those of Europe in general because Germany was perceived as a safe haven. Clearly, if you have most of your portfolio in European stocks then you would prefer to hedge your exposure using European volatility

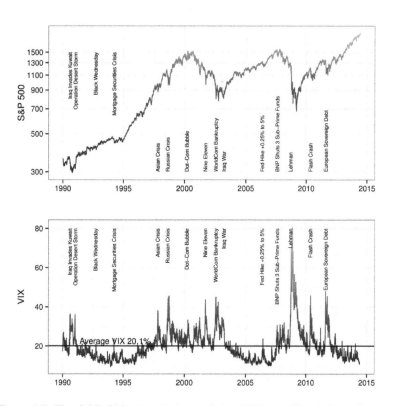

Figure 1.7: The S&P 500 share index and the VIX volatility index. Source: Bloomberg.

Volatility Index	Associated Share Index	Region
VSTOXX	EURO STOXX 50	Europe
VDAX-NEW	DAX	Germany
VHSI	Hang Seng	Hong Kong
VNKY	Nikkei 225	Japan
V-KOSPI 200	KOSPI 200	Korea
India VIX	Nifty 50	India
VSMI	SMI	Switzerland
RTSVX	RTS	Russia
SPAVIX	S&P/ASX 200	Australia
FTSE 100 IVI	FTSE 100	UK
FTSE MIB IVI	FTSE MIB	Italy
VIMEX	IPC	Mexico
VIXC	S&P/TSX 60	Canada
SAVIT40	TOP40	South Africa

Table 1.1: Regional volatility indices.

rather than US volatility. The difference between your European stock portfolio volatility and VIX is called *basis risk*. For European institutional investors whose performance is measured to hundredths of a percent VIX basis risk is unacceptable but for retail investors VIX is probably good enough.

The Risk Scale

We have seen that we can think of volatility as a measure of everyday risk. I say everyday risk because volatility is an average and this smooths out extreme events. It is useful to know the typical volatility of each investment, because this gives an idea of how much you expect to gain or lose per "typical" day. Figure 1.9 shows the range of volatility for a wide variety of investments. Notice the scale is logarithmic because if it was not the least risky investments would be invisibly small. Each dot in the graph is the annualized daily volatility measured over one month, and we plot one point for each week which gives about 400 points per investment during the period from 2005 to 2013. The width of the violin shapes shows how much time is spent by each investment at each level of volatility. The widest point is the median volatility.

By far the least volatile investments are bonds, and the safest of bonds are

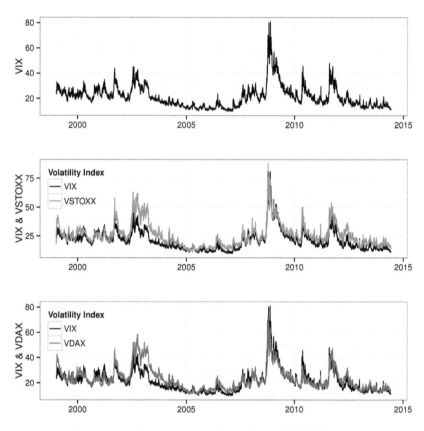

Figure 1.8: Three volatility indices: VIX (US), VSTOXX (Europe), and VDAX (Germany). Volatility for US, European and German stocks track one another closely. Source: Bloomberg.

US Treasuries. The volatility of a bond scales up with the time remaining to its maturity date such that the longer the maturity the greater the volatility. The index which we used for "US Treasury Bonds" was based on bonds which mature in a short period of time, just one to three years with an average maturity of less than two years, hence the median volatility is extremely low, just 1.4%. Slightly more risky is the more broad bond index "US Bonds" which has a longer average maturity of 6.7 years. The index we used was the Barclays Aggregate bond index which also contains more risky corporate bonds, hence with the greater maturity and credit risk we get a higher median volatility of 3.8%, about three times that of Treasuries.

Moving away from bonds into our first volatility index which we can trade as a volatility product, the S&P Dynamic VIX index, we get another jump upwards to 12.7%. The standard US share index is the S&P 500 and this sits at 15.1% on our volatility scale. Any share index in the developed markets (Europe, Japan, South Korea) would have a similar volatility. Gold, oil and single stocks, such as Google are in the 20% to 30% range. VIX is itself very volatile and tops our scale at a volatility of 99.1% which is about *seventy* times larger than the least volatile investment which is US Treasuries.

Volatility term structure

In order to understand some commonly traded volatility products it is important to understand the *term structure of volatility*. Again this is a complicated sounding name for something that is quite simple. You can either buy volatility today or you can contract to buy volatility at a fixed date in the future at a fixed price. Volatility term structure is a graph of implied volatility at a range of dates in the future, as shown in Figure 1.10. The word "term" in "term structure" means how far in the future the contract expires, and in the case of VIX the term structure is spaced in intervals of one month up to a maximum of ten months. The price of volatility on a date that is between 1 month and 4 months is called *short-term volatility*. In the middle at around 4 months to 7 months is *mid-term volatility*. The price of volatility on a date further in the future, say 8 months or more, is *long-term volatility*. Almost all trading in VIX futures is short-term and to a lesser extent mid-term.

A snapshot of VIX term structure on March 27th, 2012 is shown in Figure 1.10. On that day the term structure was steeply upward-sloping. VIX closed at a low level of 15.6% and each successive VIX future up to a term of seven months had a higher volatility, rising to 26.4% for the seven month VIX future.

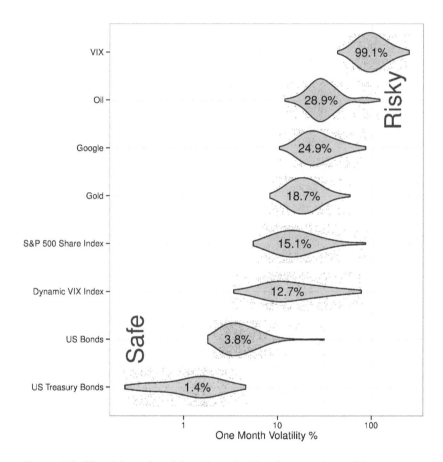

Figure 1.9: The risk scale. Monthly volatility for a variety of investments (2005 to 2013). Width of "violins" indicates number of days spent at each level of volatility. Source: Bloomberg.

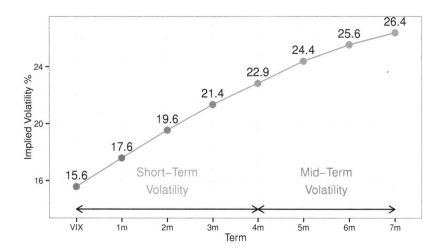

Figure 1.10: Term structure of VIX futures on March 27th, 2012. The VIX futures curve is upward-sloping which is typical of calm markets. Source: Bloomberg.

Most of the time this is how the VIX term structure curve looks, with higher implied volatility the further out in the future we look. Each day the shape and level of the VIX term structure curve changes. You can find the term structure of VIX today by looking at the CBOE web site.[4]

The shape of the term structure is a good measure of whether the market is in a state of crisis or a state of calm. When all is calm prices for short-dated volatility are smaller than long-dated volatility so the curve is upward-sloping. During a crisis investors panic and buy short-dated volatility in the belief that the crisis will worsen and short-dated volatility will increase in value. This pushes up the short end of the curve above the long end such that the term structure becomes inverted (downward-sloping). Figure 3.3 later in the book has examples of extreme changes in the shape of the VIX futures curve.

Volatility is itself volatile. Just as we can measure the volatility of an index such as the S&P 500 by measuring the typical daily change in the index, so we can measure the volatility of VIX and each VIX future. In Figure 1.11 we can see dots showing the daily closing price of VIX and each future from 2006 to 2013. Superimposed on the dots are violin shapes that show many days

---

[4]http://www.cboe.com/data/volatilityindexes

volatility closed at each level. The violins are fattest at around 20% for VIX, but for longer term VIX futures the most frequent volatility level is closer to 25%. This is because most of the time the curve is in its "normal" upward-sloping state that we saw in Figure 1.10.

What really stands out in Figure 1.11 are extreme levels because these are highest for the short-term part of the curve which reacts wildly to market shocks. If we were to characterize VIX futures as people, then VIX and the 1-month to 3-month VIX futures would be excitable teenagers and the 4-month to 7-month futures would be sedate retirees who have seen it all before. Long-dated volatility is less volatile than shorter-dated volatility. VIX products based on longer-dated futures will be less volatile, and therefore less risky, than those based on shorter-dated futures. This is why the S&P short-term VIX futures index, which is a position in 1-month and 2-month VIX futures, is more volatile than the S&P mid-term VIX futures index, which is a position in the 4-month to 7-month VIX futures.

The reason why the term structure of volatility matters is that many volatility investors trade future volatility. As we will see, many pre-packaged volatility products are in fact term structure products that pay out an amount that depends on the steepness or level of volatility term structure. Sophisticated investors such as hedge funds will be continually thinking not just about the level of overall volatility but also the steepness of the curve. If such an investor thinks we are about to enter a crisis they buy the short end of the curve and sell the long end (a *flattener* trade). Alternatively if a sophisticated investor thinks we are in the midst of crisis that is about to subside then they implicitly believe that the curve is too inverted. If this is the case the curve will steepen by falling for short-term contracts. They would express this belief by selling short-dated volatility futures and buying long-dated volatility futures (a *steepener* trade). Some volatility indices, such as the S&P dynamic VIX index even dynamically switch between flatteners and steepeners to give the best long-term return (see the section "Reducing roll cost" in Chapter 3).

Realized and implied volatility

When we work out the volatility of Google shares from a historic set of daily returns this is called *realized volatility*. As the word realized suggests, this volatility measure is backward-looking and tells us what happened in the past. When you buy volatility what you are investing in is *future* volatility, and as we all know nobody can predict the future. A buyer of volatility assumes that

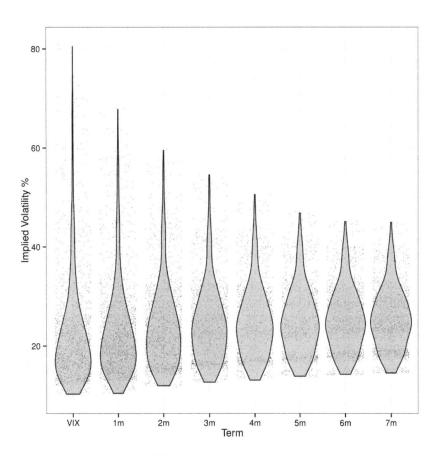

Figure 1.11: Variability of VIX term structure. Each point is the closing value of volatility for one day. Width of "violins" indicates number of days spent at a level of implied volatility. Source: Bloomberg.

volatility will be rising and on the other side of the trade the seller of volatility assumes that volatility will be falling. The price at which you buy volatility implies a future expectation for the level of volatility and this expectation is called *implied volatility*.

This is not a book about options (read my introduction to professional finance "A Financial Bestiary" if you want to know about options in detail) so I will give just the briefest description necessary. An option is the right, but not the obligation, to buy a stock at a fixed price at a fixed time in the future. The price you pay for that option depends critically on the implied volatility of a stock today. If you think about it that makes perfect sense, and an example may help.

Say it is Valentine's Day 2013 and Google is trading at $788. You buy an option to buy Google for $800 on March 16th 2013 in about one month's time. Imagine that the implied volatility of Google was zero. Zero volatility means that the market believes Google's share price will be fixed forever at $788.[5] Zero volatility would therefore mean that Google stock would *never* reach $800 and the option would be worthless. You would not exercise your option to buy Google for $800 if it is trading more cheaply in the stock market at $788.

If Google rises above $800 in March we make a profit. Say Google is worth $850 on March 16th. We would exercise our option to buy Google stock for $800, then we would sell the stock for $850 pocketing a profit of $50. The fair price of the option increases according to the expected price of Google on March 16th. More volatility increases the expected amount that the option will pay, and there is a famous formula called Black-Scholes which calculates this expected value. If we turn up the volatility dial to say 10% then according to Black-Scholes the option would gain value to $4.40. Dial up volatility to 20% and the option is now worth $12.90. This is because the price is jumping around more and therefore much more likely to cross the finishing line above our target price of $800. The important thing about Black-Scholes is that it creates a mapping between the value of the option in dollars and cents with an "implied" volatility. If you are quoted $4.40 for the March Google option then that implies a volatility of 10%.

Volatility indices such as VIX are also based on implied volatility. The way VIX is estimated is to combine implied volatility for options on S&P 500 stocks that are due to expire in roughly 30 days. VIX is therefore a measure

---

[5]This is not quite true, the zero volatility share price is the forward price which depends on interest rates and expected dividends on the stock. See "A Financial Bestiary" for details.

of volatility expected over the next 30 days. VIX is short-dated and as such it tracks realized volatility very closely. This is because over the very short-term volatility is unlikely to change much. Over the longer term there is scope for more tail events so generally longer-dated volatility tends to be higher than shorter-dated volatility. Longer-dated volatility is also less strongly correlated with realized volatility.

In Figure 1.12 we can see all these relationships. Realized S&P 500 volatility is always lowest, on average about 4% lower than VIX. There is a very close correspondence between VIX and realized volatility of the S&P 500. VIX futures also respond to the level of VIX, but their reaction becomes more muted for longer-dated futures. This is why I show the seven-month future, because it highlights the more steady nature of longer-dated VIX futures. As VIX and short-dated futures whip up and down to any piece of news the seven-month VIX future responds more slowly and sedately. This makes perfect sense because futures are based on expectations, and long-term expectations for VIX do not change much as VIX always reverts back to its 20% average.

It is important to know that implied volatility from VIX futures is not predictive. In other words if the VIX three month future is 25% that does not mean that in three months the level of VIX will be 25%. Remember that the term structure of VIX futures depends largely on the level of VIX. If VIX is high (above around 30%) the term structure usually inverts, and if VIX is "normal" at or below around 20% the term structure is steeply upward-sloping. See Figure 3.4 in section "What is roll cost?" which shows the strong relationship.

The poor predictive value of VIX futures is highlighted in Figure 1.13 which shows the volatility of VIX futures against the actual level of VIX when the future expires. Just as weather forecasts get more unreliable further out in the future, so VIX futures become very poor predictors of the future level of VIX the longer their expiry. One-month expiry futures are fairly good at predicting the level of VIX one month ahead. However note that even for the one-month VIX future many points lie far away from the red line as VIX lay far from the "predicted" value at expiry. For each successive expiry month the relationship between the predicted and actual level of VIX breaks down further. In particular the post-Lehman spike figures largely as an unforeseen event and was totally missed by six-month VIX futures.

VIX is notoriously *auto-correlated*. This simply means that if VIX is at a low value today, say 15% then it is very likely that it will be close to 15% tomorrow. If VIX is high today, say at 30%, it is likely to be high tomorrow. Of course VIX fluctuates a great deal and is itself very volatile but it does have this statistical tendency to hang around.

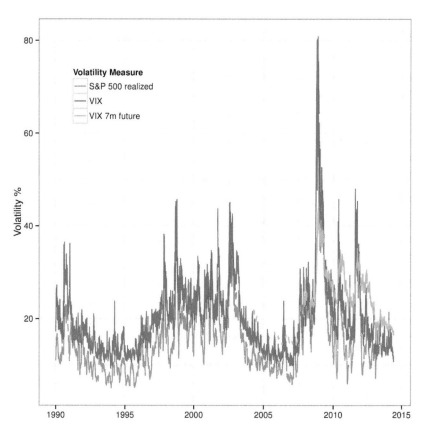

Figure 1.12: S&P 500 realized volatility (30 day window), VIX (30 day implied volatility) and VIX 7m future (implied 30 day volatility in 7 months time). Source: Bloomberg.

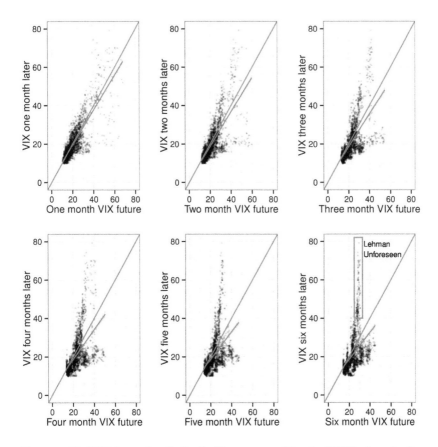

Figure 1.13: VIX future implied volatility vs. actual level of VIX when the future expires. VIX futures are poor predictors of the future value of VIX, and the predictive accuracy worsens as the forecast horizon increases. Blue line is best fit of data, red line represents a perfect prediction. Source: Bloomberg.

We can count how many days it takes for VIX to return to its long-term average of about 20.4% and the results are shown in Figure 1.14. The further VIX wanders from it's long-term average the longer it takes to return to the average but there is an interesting asymmetry. If VIX is, say, 2% above its long-term average, it returns to the average more quickly than if it is 2% below its long-term average. In other words low volatility is likely to persist longer than high volatility.

Summary

Definition Volatility is the typical daily percentage change in a price. Google's share price has a volatility of 32% which is typical for a large US company. Bond volatility is much lower, usually 2%-5% increasing with the maturity date of the bond.

Volatility has no sign Volatility investors make money when stock markets move a lot either up *or* down. They lose money when markets are quiet. An up-crash is as good as a down-crash for a volatility investor.

Implied vs Realized Realized volatility is backward-looking and calculated as the average daily variation in price. Implied volatility is forward-looking and reflects expectations about what volatility will be at a fixed date in the future.

Stock market crashes Crashes in stock price make volatility jump higher. Steady and prolonged stock market rallies make volatility fall.

Hedging By buying an exchange traded product linked to volatility it is possible to reduce the risk of volatility in a stock portfolio in two ways: (i) this cushions the blow from stock market crashes and (ii) counteracts the daily volatility of the stocks in your portfolio.

VIX This is the "fear index" which measures US stock market volatility. In Europe the volatility indices are VSTOXX and VDAX. VIX is mean-reverting which means it always returns to its long-term average of about 20%, unlike stock indices which tend to continually drift upwards.

Term Structure of Volatility VIX futures allow investors to buy future volatility at a fixed price at a fixed time in the future. The price of future volatility from one month to nine months in future defines the "term structure" of volatility.

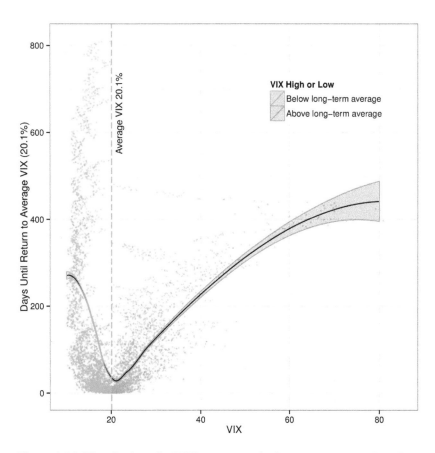

Figure 1.14: Time in days for VIX to revert to its long-term average based on the level of VIX today. Source: Bloomberg.

Roll Cost Long-term VIX futures are usually more expensive than short-term VIX futures which means that maintaining a position in VIX futures continually loses money. This is called roll cost, and rapidly erodes the value of some VIX exchange traded products.

2 A brief history of volatility

> In reading the history of nations, we find that, like individuals, they have their whims and their peculiarities; their seasons of excitement and recklessness, when they care not what they do. We find that whole communities suddenly fix their minds upon one object, and go mad in its pursuit; that millions of people become simultaneously impressed with one delusion, and run after it, till their attention is caught by some new folly more captivating than the first. We see one nation suddenly seized, from its highest to its lowest members, with a fierce desire of military glory; another as suddenly becoming crazed upon a religious scruple; and neither of them recovering its senses until it has shed rivers of blood and sowed a harvest of groans and tears, to be reaped by its posterity.

> *Preface to "Memoirs of Extraordinary Popular Delusions and the Madness of Crowds" by Charles Mackay.*

Reading this chapter will show you which events drove volatility higher and lower in the past. Notice that volatility usually does the opposite of the stock market, so if share prices are rising volatility tends to be low and when stock prices fall volatility jumps higher. For each crisis I have shown the impact on the stock market as well as the VIX index.

We begin with a summary of the volatility drivers that turn up repeatedly. A more detailed list of volatility events in chronological order then follows later in the chapter.

Valuation Bubbles Stock market rallies tend to overshoot beyond reasonable valuations. During a rally volatility is very low, as we saw in the strong rallies from 1992-1997 and 2003-2007. The inevitable market correction causes share prices to tumble quickly and volatility to spike as occurred when the dot-com bubble burst in 2000 and the sub-prime property bubble burst in 2008 leading to the Credit Crisis.

War Generally increases VIX but only if it affects US corporate earnings. Because the US has a huge oil appetite, war in the Middle East is disproportionately important as it increases all crude oil prices (such as West Texas Intermediate and Brent Crude). Sometimes war reduces volatility, as occurred in the US invasion of Iraq in 2003 after which stocks rallied and volatility tumbled. This is because the outcome of the war, which toppled the regime of Saddam Hussein, was seen as securing the supply of oil and creating political stability in the Middle East which was interpreted by markets as positive news. Over the coming decades the importance of the Middle East to US equity volatility will wane as US shale oil production increases and the US reduces its imports and potentially becomes a net oil exporter.

Recession Recession[1] usually means corporate earnings and stock prices will fall and volatility will be higher. The US central bank, the Federal Reserve cuts interest rates during a recession to make the cost of borrowing cheaper for businesses and individuals and to stimulate growth. Fed monetary policy played a large part in stemming the Russian Crisis in 1998 with such a rate cut. Conversely if the economy is overheating and inflation is starting to rise the Fed usually raises interest rates. Some compare this to taking away the punch bowl when a party becomes too rowdy. As the Fed hikes rates stock markets tend to fall and volatility rises, as occurred in 1994. Sometimes more extreme unconventional policy is required. Following the Credit Crisis the Federal Reserve provided massive amounts of liquidity in a program of quantitative easing where it bought huge amounts of US Treasuries and mortgage products to push down long-term interest rates. This eventually reversed the fall in equity markets and pushed down volatility.

Bankruptcies Small companies file for bankruptcy all the time without affecting the VIX index. VIX is an aggregate measure of volatility based on the volatility of the 500 largest US companies which compose the S&P 500 share index. On the rare occasion when a large company files for bankruptcy, such as WorldCom in 2002 and Lehman Brothers in 2008, this is usually a sign of bigger problems. WorldCom exposed some questionable accounting practices used to inflate asset values and share prices, and Lehman Brothers exposed excessive risk-taking by investment banks.

---

[1] Recession is defined roughly as two successive quarters of falling GDP. For the exact definition from the US National Bureau of Economic Research see http://www.nber.org/cycles/recessions_faq.html.

Politics Although politicians have a poor record with reducing volatility US presidents can very easily increase it through the three D's: disease, death, or disgrace. Examples include President Eisenhower's heart attack in 1955, President Kennedy's assassination in 1963 and President Nixon's ignominious departure in 1974. A veritable Old Faithful geyser of politically induced volatility is the US debt ceiling where partisan squabbles erupt each time the ceiling has to be raised. In August 2011 stock markets tumbled as this disagreement flared yet again. Protests against the government can sometimes be so violent that they affect the stock market, as occurred following the Kent State Shootings in 1970 when President Nixon had to be evacuated to Camp David for his own safety.

Terrorism The 911 attacks in 2001 caused a brief spike in volatility but the effect was modest and short-lived compared to the Credit Crisis. This attack was aimed at disrupting the US financial system as the Twin Towers in New York contained the offices of many investment banks, so it was in some sense a worst case for volatility. Other occurrences of domestic terrorism in the US such as the bombing of the Federal Building in April 1995 or the Boston Marathon bombings in April 2013 did not affect volatility.

Natural Disasters If a natural disaster affects US companies, either through exports falling or the price of imports rising, then VIX will rise. For example the Japanese Tohoku Earthquake, Tsunami and subsequent nuclear disaster in Fukushima in 2011 disrupted supply chains which affected US companies. Volatility could be driven higher by global pandemics but this has not happened in developed markets in living memory and would have to incapacitate a large fraction of the US population or consumers of US products outside the US in order to drive up market volatility. Events such as tornadoes, hurricanes, floods, volcanic eruptions and earthquakes are usually localized and so generally do not affect volatility. It would take a cataclysmic global natural disaster such as a large meteor strike in a populated area or eruption of a super-volcano in order to drive volatility higher.

Flash Crashes The Flash Crash in 2010 was a widely attributed to a rapid negative feedback cycle where computer algorithms amplified a negative price blip into a full-blown market crash. Although stabilization mechanisms are are in place to avoid this recurring there is no guarantee this will not happen again. This was not the first time this had happened. A flash crash occurred in 1962 long before algorithmic trading existed and left investors, journalists and the Securities and Exchange Commission unable to find the cause. The severe global stock market crash on Black Monday in 1987 may fall into this category too. These events resemble clear air turbulence in that they are sudden, unpredictable, and seem to come out of the blue.

Use events to time your trades

To make good profits with volatility investments you need to time your trades well. There are some people who are good at knowing when to buy volatility and some who are good at knowing when to sell volatility but very few people are good at both. For example some pundits have their barometer stuck in crisis mode all the time, and occasionally they are proven spectacularly correct. They then gain media attention with "I told you so" interviews. But almost all the time the signals from such Dr Doom pundits will be wrong and will lose money if you take a long volatility position because crises are, by their nature, extremely rare. Other pundits are continually bullish telling investors to buy equities. Given that equities drift upwards over the very long term these people are more likely to be correct, but as an equity investor you should be willing to lose 50% of your money some of the time unless you invest in volatility.

Use this chapter as a starting point in your own research to see what initiates and what ends financial crises. If you can time both ends of a crisis you will perform very well indeed with your volatility trades. Crises are sometimes just forgotten, and these are the hardest crises to time your exit because no definitive event causes a fall in VIX. In these cases you might want to develop a strategy such as the ones given in Chapter 4.

Volatility Before VIX

Although VIX is calculated starting in 1990 it is possible to calculate one-month realized volatility for the S&P 500 as far back as daily time series are available, which is around 1950. If you're scratching your head and wondering what "realized volatility" means, see the section "Realized and implied volatility" in Chapter 1 for the definition and the difference between realized and implied volatility.

Historically VIX tracks one-month realized S&P 500 volatility very closely but with 4% extra volatility. Even if we add 4%, the period from 1950 to just before the 1987 crash was one of extremely low volatility. The average realized volatility was 11.6%, comparable to a VIX volatility of 15.6%. The average level of VIX since 1990 has been over 20%. It may be that the postwar boom was unusually peaceful and that we have to live with a more volatile world, in which case it makes a lot of sense to invest in volatility.

Broadly speaking the period between 1950 and 1970 was a strong equity rally punctuated with war-related crises in Asia related to the Cold War (see Figure 2.1). From the point of view of volatility this was a quiet period. From 1970 to 1980 equities were largely flat with oil and inflation driving volatility spikes. From 1980 to 1990 there was another strong rally with low volatility as inflation fell and growth returned. However 1987 stands out as a sudden market shock resembling the flash crashes in 1962 and 2010, and in terms of volatility it set a record that would not be exceeded until the Credit Crisis two decades later. In the text below the acronyms in bold explain the equivalent labels shown in Figure 2.1.

1950 KorWar *Outbreak of Korean War* In June 1950 the Korean War began. Although much smaller in scale than WWII the outbreak of war between North and South Korea was sufficient to reduce the S&P 500 by about 13% over the course of June and July and to double volatility from 13% to over 30%. After WWII the Allies had agreed to divide Korea along the 38th parallel with Soviet forces occupying the North and US forces occupying the South. On June 25th North Korea invaded the South, an action that was condemned by the United Nations which organized an armed force to repel the invasion with the US providing the majority of the 340,000 troops. UN Command forces quickly pushed the invading force back to the 38th parallel.

1950 ChKorWar *China Enters Korean War* In October 1950 the Chinese joined the war supporting North Korea. Chinese and US forces engaged in the Korean War for the first time on November 1st 1950. This pushed volatility up again to a smaller peak of around 26% in November and December. UN command forces were forced to retreat from north-west Korea and after several pitched battles the war entered a stalemate around the 38th parallel. By 1951 volatility had fallen to its average level and was oblivious to the War which officially ended with the armistice agreement of July 27th 1953.

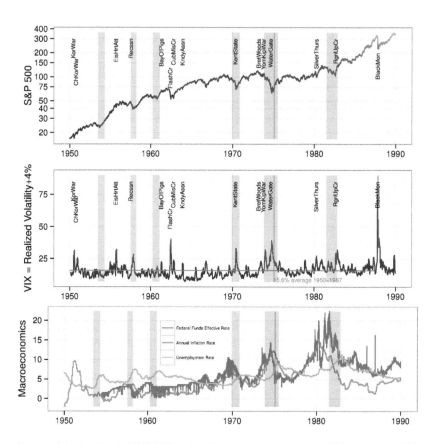

Figure 2.1: Realized S&P 500 volatility (+4% to emulate VIX) before 1990 with Fed Funds effective rate, US year-on-year inflation and US unemployment rate. Shaded regions are US recessions as defined by the National Bureau of Economic Research. Source: Bloomberg. and Federal Reserve Bank of St. Louis.

1955 EisHrtAtt *Eisenhower Heart Attack* On September 24th 1955 US President Dwight Eisenhower suffered a heart attack while on holiday in Colorado which required six weeks hospitalization. Stocks fell by 11% over the next two weeks and volatility tripled from 11% to 33% but the effect of this shocking news was short-lived and the President recovered.

1957 Recssn *Recession* The US went into recession in August 1957 from which it emerged eight months later. Unemployment reached new highs not seen since the war, industrial production (such as steel, oil and car production) slowed during this period and stock prices fell as a result. As is still the case Republicans and Democrats disagreed on the solution, with Republicans calling for tax cuts and Democrats for increased spending. As a result stocks slumped and there was a period of prolonged high volatility lasting from August 1957 until January 1958.

1961 BayOfPigs *Bay of Pigs Invasion* On April 17th 1961 a US backed counter-revolutionary force failed to overthrow Fidel Castro's Cuban government. The US at the time saw a communist state on its doorstep as a security threat. This failed military action backfired as it embarrassed the Kennedy administration, increased Castro's popularity in Cuba and may have been responsible for strengthening Cuba's links with the Soviet Union which later led to the Cuban missile crisis. As a result the stock market fell slightly and volatility rose from around 12% to 22% during May 1961.

1962 FlashCr *Flash Crash* On May 28th 1962 markets fell for no particular reason foreshadowing the flash crash of 2010, leaving market participants dazed. Volatility quadrupled from 10% to over 40% and remained high for over a month after the event. The Dow Jones fell 5.7% in one day and the S&P 500 fell 6.7%, the second-worst single-day fall on record at that time. Traded volume was so high that the ticker wasn't able to finish reporting floor transactions until six in the evening, over two hours after the market closed. Blue-chip shares like IBM tumbled by 5.3% over the course of 19 minutes and smaller companies fared worse. What is interesting is that this occurred decades before the existence of high-frequency trading which was blamed for the 2010 Flash Crash. An inconclusive SEC report on the event published a year later stated[2] that:

---

[2] See http://www.sechistorical.org/collection/papers/1960/1963_SSMkt_Chapter_13_1.pdf.

"The markets' erratic behavior prompted concern and caused bewilderment at home and abroad. The frenetic activity of the break resulted in large and sudden losses for many and gains for some... this break had a strong and immediate psychological impact upon the Nation."

1962 CubMisCr *Cuban Missile Crisis* On October 15th 1962 the US published pictures clearly showing the construction of nuclear missile launch sites in Cuba. This event is considered to be the closest that the US and Soviet Union came to a nuclear conflict. The crisis lasted just two weeks during which the US Navy tried to blockade Soviet ships from accessing Cuba. As a blockade is officially an act of war it was described as a "quarantine". Eventually both sides backed down and on October 27th the US agreed to remove its own missiles from Italy and Turkey and in response Khrushchev removed the Soviet missiles from Cuba. Volatility remained high from mid-October to December 1962 .

1963 KndyAssn *Kennedy Assassination* On November 22nd 1963 President John F. Kennedy was shot by a lone gunman Lee Harvey Oswald while visiting Dallas in Texas. Given that this was the height of the Cold War there were concerns that the Soviet Union was behind the attack and that the vice president Lyndon Johnson was also injured. Lyndon Johnson was not injured and was sworn in aboard Air Force One just a few hours after Kennedy's death. Coming as it did during a red-hot rally in equity from 1962 to 1968 the assassination-induced volatility was short-lived despite global outpouring of grief and shock at the event.

1970 KentState *Kent State Shootings* On April 30th US President Richard Nixon announced that the US would be would be invading Cambodia in order to defeat Vietnamese troops who were camped on the eastern border adjoining Vietnam. Nixon had been elected on a policy of ending the Vietnam War and many saw this as a backwards step in the process. In particular students who faced the draft were opposed to the move and a series of student protests broke out resulting in the Kent State shootings on May 4th. The Ohio National Guard opened fire on unarmed protesters killing four students and injuring nine others. There were fierce demonstrations in Washington D.C. following the shootings and Nixon had to be taken to Camp David for his own protection. Combined with a recession and the highest inflation for a decade this sequence of events triggered a sharp equity sell-off and volatility increased.

1973/1974 *Recession & Bear Market* Between January 1973 and October 1974 the S&P 500 fell by 48%. While share prices halved volatility quadrupled from around 10% to over 40%. Inflation tripled from around 3% to 12% and the recession lasted from November 1973 to March 1975. This bear market and the recession that came with it marked the end of a spectacular share rally that began after the Second World War. The share sell-off and rising volatility came in three waves that could be summarized as the **dollar-spike** (January-September 1973) as the link between the price of gold and the dollar was broken with the demise of Bretton Woods, the **oil-spike** (November 1973 to March 1974) as the Arab-Israeli conflict flared, and the **political-spike** (July 1974 to April 1975) caused by the Watergate scandal that led to the resignation of President Nixon.

March 1973 BretWoods *The End of Bretton Woods* From 1944 to 1973 there had been a system of fixed exchange rates between major currencies and the dollar. The dollar itself was fixed relative to the price of gold at a rate of $35 per ounce. In 1944 the US held 65% of the global total of $40 billion in gold reserves. Bretton Woods, named after the area in New Hampshire where it was agreed, was intended to avoid countries trying to competitively devalue their own currency to boost exports. This policy is called "beggar thy neighbour" devaluation and was used destructively during and after the Great Depression of the 1930s and 1940s. By fixing exchange rates to one another and founding the entire system on the dollar value of gold the delegates at Bretton Woods were putting an end to beggar thy neighbour policies. By 1973 there was huge pressure on the US to end the system as its gold reserves dwindled, inflation rose and its balance of trade swung into a deep deficit. Individual countries started to leave the peg to the dollar and by March 1973 the agreement ended and currencies could float freely relative to one another and the value of the dollar and gold were no longer linked. Volatility rose as a result and stock markets sold off from January to August 1973.

October 1973 YomKipWar *Yom Kippur War & Arab Oil Embargo* On October 6th 1973 Israel was simultaneously attacked by Egypt (from the south-west) and Syria (from the north-east) in an attempt to regain land captured and occupied by Israel in Sinai and the Golan Heights during the 1967 Six Day War. Israeli forces quickly repelled the invasion and drove beyond the pre-war borders deep into both Egyptian and Syrian territory. Superpowers were indirectly involved, with the US backing Israel and the Soviet Union backing Egypt and Syria. Initially markets in the US did not react as this was seen as a regional conflict which ended in stalemate on October 25th. However in response to the Yom Kippur War middle-eastern oil producers announced an immediate increase in the price of oil by 17% and a reduction in production. Several major oil producers announced an oil embargo on exports to the United States after Nixon requested Congress to approve a $2.2 billion dollar aid package for Israel on October 19th. As the price of oil surged share prices fell and volatility increased steadily until the end of 1973.

August 1974 WaterGate *Watergate* On August 8th 1974 President Richard Nixon announced his resignation after it emerged that he had lied about a cover-up following a break-in to Democratic Party offices in the Watergate office complex in Washington D.C. in June 1972. Cash found on the burglars was linked to Nixon's re-election campaign fund. Tape recordings made in the White House showed that the president was not only aware of illegal actions carried out after the break-in but also responsible for the cover-up. He is heard on the tapes saying that he wanted the CIA to falsely claim to the FBI that national security was involved. Eventually this led to imprisonment for many government officials for charges including obstruction of justice, perjury, wiretapping, and burglary. The list of those convicted included two US Attorney Generals and many White House staffers.

1980 SilverThurs *Silver Thursday* The price of silver and US share prices fell sharply on March 27th 1980. The panic was caused by brothers Nelson and William Hunt who had cornered the market in silver, hoarding one third of the global supply. This led to a sharp rise in the price of silver from $5 an ounce at the end of the 1970s to a peak of $50. The Hunt brothers had borrowed money to fund their massive investment, and when the government changed the law to limit leverage they were forced to sell at a catastrophic loss. This rattled other markets because it was possible that brokerage firms and banks involved in the Hunt brothers silver transactions could have become insolvent. This contagion was avoided when a group of banks loaned over a billion dollars to the brothers to allow them to settle their losses. The S&P 500 fell 17% from February to the end of March and realized volatility rose from 10% to 23%.

1982 RgnUpCr *Reagan Up-Crash* Sometimes markets crash upwards as well as downwards, and because volatility is blind to direction either will boost its value. Reagan was elected as President in 1981 with a policy of free markets, small government and anti-communism. He inherited an economy of very high inflation (over 10%) and high unemployment (over 7%) and, teamed with Paul Volcker as Chairman of the Federal Reserve, transformed this into low inflation, rising employment and good economic growth. The inflection point as the cosh of inflation was removed created a sudden rally of +66% in the S&P 500 from August 1982 to June 1983. Because this was a sudden, sharp rally with very high trading volume it increased realized volatility on August 17th from 12% to 26% and this period of high volatility lasted for eight months.

1987 BlackMon *Black Monday Crash* On October 19, 1987 stock markets in Asia fell sharply and chaos spread westward. The S&P 500 fell from 314.52 on October 13th to 224.84 on October 19th, a fall of 29%, with a 20% fall on Monday 19th, which became known as Black Monday. As each market opened, first in Europe then the US they crashed in turn. The 1987 crash set a record for volatility at the time, reaching Lehman-like levels of realized volatility of around 80%. Like the other flash crashes of 1962 and 2010 the cause is disputed. Many blame program trading, which is automated trading of several stocks at the same time. However the global sell-off in shares started in Hong Kong where there was little or no program trading so this cannot be the sole cause. In London there was a severe storm on October 15-16 which led to many traders being absent from work in the days leading up to the crash, but again this is a localized issue which can't explain falls in other markets.

VIX before the Credit Crisis

Data for the VIX index starts in 1990 and in this section we will focus on events from 1990 to just before the Credit Crisis in 2007. This was an extremely bountiful twenty years for the US equity market. There were just two brief US recessions, one in 1990/1991 and another following the bursting of the dot-com bubble in 2001. From 1992 until 2000 equities rose steadily with an acceleration in 1995. Volatility flipped from a low-ish 14% (1991-1997) to a high-ish 25% (1997-2003) then back to a low-ish 16% (2003-2007) as the equity market rallied, traded sideways, stalled and fell after the dot-com bubble, then rallied again. The step-up in volatility in 1997 coincided with the Asian crisis, and what is interesting is that despite higher volatility the equity market continued to rally, albeit with a tumble during the Russian crisis, right up to March 2000.

1990 IraqInvKwt *Iraq Invades Kuwait* On August 2nd 1990 Iraq invaded and annexed Kuwait. As Iraq and Kuwait are major oil producers and the US was a big importer of foreign oil, the sharp rise in the price of oil after this event was a drag on US corporate earnings. The link between war in the Middle East and volatility is through the dependency of the United States on oil. If the US manages to produce enough oil to be self-sufficient the link between political instability in the Middle East and volatility will be much weaker. But for now, and certainly in 1990, the link was strong. Following the invasion the S&P 500 fell 19% and volatility jumped from 15% to 37% (see Figure 2.3).

1991 OpDesStorm *Operation Desert Storm* On January 17th 1991 the US began a shock and awe bombing campaign that was carried on live television throughout the World. As it became clear that the US would be able to force Iraq out of Kuwait thanks to its overwhelming air superiority, markets quickly recovered. The S&P 500 rallied by 28% from its post-invasion low and VIX fell back to 15%.

1992 BlackWed *Black Wednesday* On September 16th 1992 speculators created instability and volatility in the currency markets centred around the British pound. Before the existence of the euro Britain had decided to be part of the European Exchange Rate Mechanism (ERM) which attempted to keep European currencies within narrow bands with one another as a way of keeping currency volatility low to help European trade. Currency speculators believed that the value at which sterling entered the ERM was too high and sold the pound versus the Deutsche Mark and other European currencies. Although the British Treasury tried to counteract the sales by using up its reserves to buy sterling the speculators won and Britain was forced to exit the ERM. The hedge fund manager George Soros allegedly made over a billion dollars by shorting sterling. In Figure 2.4 notice that the effect on both the S&P 500 (6%

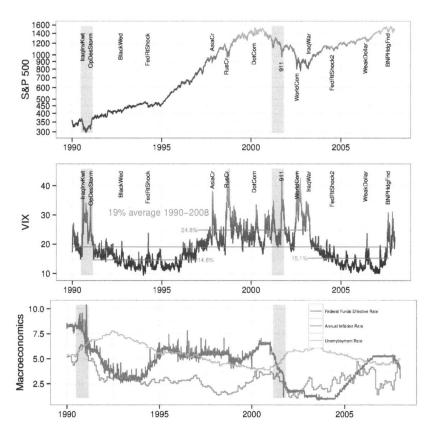

Figure 2.2: VIX from its inception in 1990 to 2007 with Fed Funds effective rate, US year-on-year inflation and US unemployment rate. Shaded regions are US recessions as defined by the National Bureau of Economic Research. Source: Bloomberg. and Federal Reserve Bank of St. Louis.

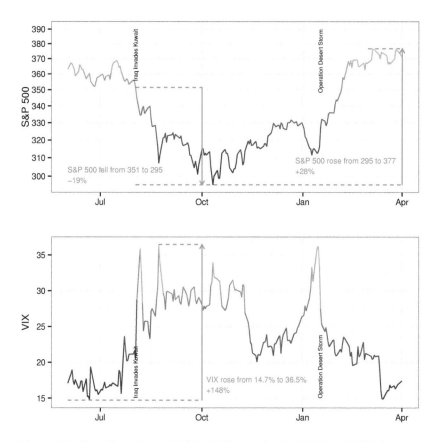

Figure 2.3: The effect of the 1990 Gulf War on the S&P 500 and VIX. Source: Bloomberg.

fall) and VIX (rose from 12.3% to 21%) was small despite the dramatic fall in the sterling to Deutsche Mark exchange rate (GBPDEM), because this was seen as a British problem not a US problem.

1994 FedRtShock *Interest Rate Shocks* The Federal Reserve shocked markets by sharply raising its Fed funds rate on February 4th from 3% to 3.25% for the first time in five years. On March 22nd another rate hike followed raising the rate to 3.5%. It is interesting that the biggest tumble in stock prices happened after the second rate hike, with a total fall of 10% in the S&P 500 and a surge in volatility from 9.9% to 23.9%. Further rate hikes followed in April, May, August and November which brought the Fed funds rate to 5.5% at the close of the year. This caused havoc in bond markets which sold off sharply. Fixed rate mortgages exceeded 8.5% compared to 6.8% in October 1993. The sharp rise in interest rates led to the bankruptcy of Orange County in December when its portfolio of interest rate derivatives, which assumed that rates would stay low, took a massive loss.

1997 AsiaCr *Asian Crisis* In 1997 Thailand's government had borrowed heavily, its foreign currency reserves were exhausted and it could no longer maintain the peg between its currency, the Thai baht, to the US dollar. On July 2nd the Thai baht peg of 25 to the dollar broke and the currency devalued rapidly by a half and Thai stocks fell by 75%. What followed was a process of contagion whereby other Asian countries with sound economic fundamentals also had their currencies devalue and their stock markets tumble. US markets ignored the situation until October 27th when US stocks fell so sharply in one day (the Dow Jones Industrial Average fell 7.2%) that the New York Stock Exchange briefly suspended trading. In the next few days the VIX doubled from 18% to 38% (see Figure 2.6).

1998 RusCr *Russian Crisis* Following the Asian Crisis the price of oil and industrial metals fell both of which are important sources of income for the Russian economy. Government spending remained high and the ruble was pegged to foreign currencies at a high rate. On August 17th 1998 the Russian government defaulted on its domestic debt, said it would defer payments on foreign debt and devalued the ruble. A month

Roll Cost Long-term VIX futures are usually more expensive than short-term VIX futures which means that maintaining a position in VIX futures continually loses money. This is called roll cost, and rapidly erodes the value of some VIX exchange traded products.

portionately important as it increases all crude oil prices (such as West Texas Intermediate and Brent Crude). Sometimes war reduces volatility, as occurred in the US invasion of Iraq in 2003 after which stocks rallied and volatility tumbled. This is because the outcome of the war, which toppled the regime of Saddam Hussein, was seen as securing the supply of oil and creating political stability in the Middle East which was interpreted by markets as positive news. Over the coming decades the importance of the Middle East to US equity volatility will wane as US shale oil production increases and the US reduces its imports and potentially becomes a net oil exporter.

Recession Recession[1] usually means corporate earnings and stock prices will fall and volatility will be higher. The US central bank, the Federal Reserve cuts interest rates during a recession to make the cost of borrowing cheaper for businesses and individuals and to stimulate growth. Fed monetary policy played a large part in stemming the Russian Crisis in 1998 with such a rate cut. Conversely if the economy is overheating and inflation is starting to rise the Fed usually raises interest rates. Some compare this to taking away the punch bowl when a party becomes too rowdy. As the Fed hikes rates stock markets tend to fall and volatility rises, as occurred in 1994. Sometimes more extreme unconventional policy is required. Following the Credit Crisis the Federal Reserve provided massive amounts of liquidity in a program of quantitative easing where it bought huge amounts of US Treasuries and mortgage products to push down long-term interest rates. This eventually reversed the fall in equity markets and pushed down volatility.

Bankruptcies Small companies file for bankruptcy all the time without affecting the VIX index. VIX is an aggregate measure of volatility based on the volatility of the 500 largest US companies which compose the S&P 500 share index. On the rare occasion when a large company files for bankruptcy, such as WorldCom in 2002 and Lehman Brothers in 2008, this is usually a sign of bigger problems. WorldCom exposed some questionable accounting practices used to inflate asset values and share prices, and Lehman Brothers exposed excessive risk-taking by investment banks.

---

[1] Recession is defined roughly as two successive quarters of falling GDP. For the exact definition from the US National Bureau of Economic Research see http://www.nber.org/cycles/recessions_faq.html.

this will not happen again. This was not the first time this had happened. A flash crash occurred in 1962 long before algorithmic trading existed and left investors, journalists and the Securities and Exchange Commission unable to find the cause. The severe global stock market crash on Black Monday in 1987 may fall into this category too. These events resemble clear air turbulence in that they are sudden, unpredictable, and seem to come out of the blue.

Use events to time your trades

To make good profits with volatility investments you need to time your trades well. There are some people who are good at knowing when to buy volatility and some who are good at knowing when to sell volatility but very few people are good at both. For example some pundits have their barometer stuck in crisis mode all the time, and occasionally they are proven spectacularly correct. They then gain media attention with "I told you so" interviews. But almost all the time the signals from such Dr Doom pundits will be wrong and will lose money if you take a long volatility position because crises are, by their nature, extremely rare. Other pundits are continually bullish telling investors to buy equities. Given that equities drift upwards over the very long term these people are more likely to be correct, but as an equity investor you should be willing to lose 50% of your money some of the time unless you invest in volatility.

Use this chapter as a starting point in your own research to see what initiates and what ends financial crises. If you can time both ends of a crisis you will perform very well indeed with your volatility trades. Crises are sometimes just forgotten, and these are the hardest crises to time your exit because no definitive event causes a fall in VIX. In these cases you might want to develop a strategy such as the ones given in Chapter 4.

Volatility Before VIX

Although VIX is calculated starting in 1990 it is possible to calculate one-month realized volatility for the S&P 500 as far back as daily time series are available, which is around 1950. If you're scratching your head and wondering what "realized volatility" means, see the section "Realized and implied volatility" in Chapter 1 for the definition and the difference between realized and implied volatility.

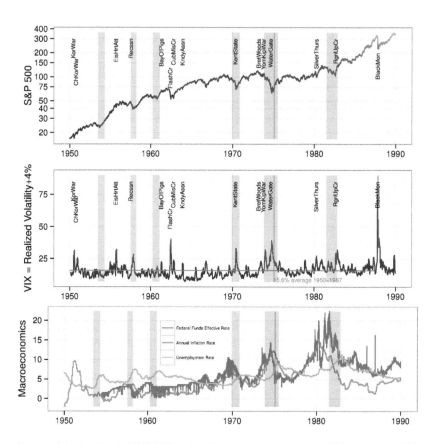

Figure 2.1: Realized S&P 500 volatility (+4% to emulate VIX) before 1990 with Fed Funds effective rate, US year-on-year inflation and US unemployment rate. Shaded regions are US recessions as defined by the National Bureau of Economic Research. Source: Bloomberg. and Federal Reserve Bank of St. Louis.

"The markets' erratic behavior prompted concern and caused bewilderment at home and abroad. The frenetic activity of the break resulted in large and sudden losses for many and gains for some... this break had a strong and immediate psychological impact upon the Nation."

1962 CubMisCr *Cuban Missile Crisis* On October 15th 1962 the US published pictures clearly showing the construction of nuclear missile launch sites in Cuba. This event is considered to be the closest that the US and Soviet Union came to a nuclear conflict. The crisis lasted just two weeks during which the US Navy tried to blockade Soviet ships from accessing Cuba. As a blockade is officially an act of war it was described as a "quarantine". Eventually both sides backed down and on October 27th the US agreed to remove its own missiles from Italy and Turkey and in response Khrushchev removed the Soviet missiles from Cuba. Volatility remained high from mid-October to December 1962 .

1963 KndyAssn *Kennedy Assassination* On November 22nd 1963 President John F. Kennedy was shot by a lone gunman Lee Harvey Oswald while visiting Dallas in Texas. Given that this was the height of the Cold War there were concerns that the Soviet Union was behind the attack and that the vice president Lyndon Johnson was also injured. Lyndon Johnson was not injured and was sworn in aboard Air Force One just a few hours after Kennedy's death. Coming as it did during a red-hot rally in equity from 1962 to 1968 the assassination-induced volatility was short-lived despite global outpouring of grief and shock at the event.

1970 KentState *Kent State Shootings* On April 30th US President Richard Nixon announced that the US would be would be invading Cambodia in order to defeat Vietnamese troops who were camped on the eastern border adjoining Vietnam. Nixon had been elected on a policy of ending the Vietnam War and many saw this as a backwards step in the process. In particular students who faced the draft were opposed to the move and a series of student protests broke out resulting in the Kent State shootings on May 4th. The Ohio National Guard opened fire on unarmed protesters killing four students and injuring nine others. There were fierce demonstrations in Washington D.C. following the shootings and Nixon had to be taken to Camp David for his own protection. Combined with a recession and the highest inflation for a decade this sequence of events triggered a sharp equity sell-off and volatility increased.

repelled the invasion and drove beyond the pre-war borders deep into both Egyptian and Syrian territory. Superpowers were indirectly involved, with the US backing Israel and the Soviet Union backing Egypt and Syria. Initially markets in the US did not react as this was seen as a regional conflict which ended in stalemate on October 25th. However in response to the Yom Kippur War middle-eastern oil producers announced an immediate increase in the price of oil by 17% and a reduction in production. Several major oil producers announced an oil embargo on exports to the United States after Nixon requested Congress to approve a $2.2 billion dollar aid package for Israel on October 19th. As the price of oil surged share prices fell and volatility increased steadily until the end of 1973.

August 1974 WaterGate *Watergate* On August 8th 1974 President Richard Nixon announced his resignation after it emerged that he had lied about a cover-up following a break-in to Democratic Party offices in the Watergate office complex in Washington D.C. in June 1972. Cash found on the burglars was linked to Nixon's re-election campaign fund. Tape recordings made in the White House showed that the president was not only aware of illegal actions carried out after the break-in but also responsible for the cover-up. He is heard on the tapes saying that he wanted the CIA to falsely claim to the FBI that national security was involved. Eventually this led to imprisonment for many government officials for charges including obstruction of justice, perjury, wiretapping, and burglary. The list of those convicted included two US Attorney Generals and many White House staffers.

1980 SilverThurs *Silver Thursday* The price of silver and US share prices fell sharply on March 27th 1980. The panic was caused by brothers Nelson and William Hunt who had cornered the market in silver, hoarding one third of the global supply. This led to a sharp rise in the price of silver from $5 an ounce at the end of the 1970s to a peak of $50. The Hunt brothers had borrowed money to fund their massive investment, and when the government changed the law to limit leverage they were forced to sell at a catastrophic loss. This rattled other markets because it was possible that brokerage firms and banks involved in the Hunt brothers silver transactions could have become insolvent. This contagion was avoided when a group of banks loaned over a billion dollars to the broth-

an acceleration in 1995. Volatility flipped from a low-ish 14% (1991-1997) to a high-ish 25% (1997-2003) then back to a low-ish 16% (2003-2007) as the equity market rallied, traded sideways, stalled and fell after the dot-com bubble, then rallied again. The step-up in volatility in 1997 coincided with the Asian crisis, and what is interesting is that despite higher volatility the equity market continued to rally, albeit with a tumble during the Russian crisis, right up to March 2000.

1990 IraqInvKwt *Iraq Invades Kuwait* On August 2nd 1990 Iraq invaded and annexed Kuwait. As Iraq and Kuwait are major oil producers and the US was a big importer of foreign oil, the sharp rise in the price of oil after this event was a drag on US corporate earnings. The link between war in the Middle East and volatility is through the dependency of the United States on oil. If the US manages to produce enough oil to be self-sufficient the link between political instability in the Middle East and volatility will be much weaker. But for now, and certainly in 1990, the link was strong. Following the invasion the S&P 500 fell 19% and volatility jumped from 15% to 37% (see Figure 2.3).

1991 OpDesStorm *Operation Desert Storm* On January 17th 1991 the US began a shock and awe bombing campaign that was carried on live television throughout the World. As it became clear that the US would be able to force Iraq out of Kuwait thanks to its overwhelming air superiority, markets quickly recovered. The S&P 500 rallied by 28% from its post-invasion low and VIX fell back to 15%.

1992 BlackWed *Black Wednesday* On September 16th 1992 speculators created instability and volatility in the currency markets centred around the British pound. Before the existence of the euro Britain had decided to be part of the European Exchange Rate Mechanism (ERM) which attempted to keep European currencies within narrow bands with one another as a way of keeping currency volatility low to help European trade. Currency speculators believed that the value at which sterling entered the ERM was too high and sold the pound versus the Deutsche Mark and other European currencies. Although the British Treasury tried to counteract the sales by using up its reserves to buy sterling the speculators won and Britain was forced to exit the ERM. The hedge fund manager George Soros allegedly made over a billion dollars by shorting sterling. In Figure 2.4 notice that the effect on both the S&P 500 (6%

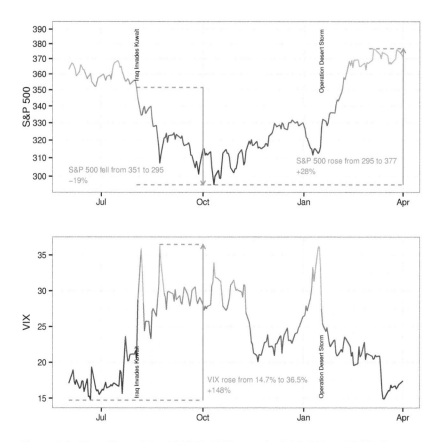

Figure 2.3: The effect of the 1990 Gulf War on the S&P 500 and VIX. Source: Bloomberg.

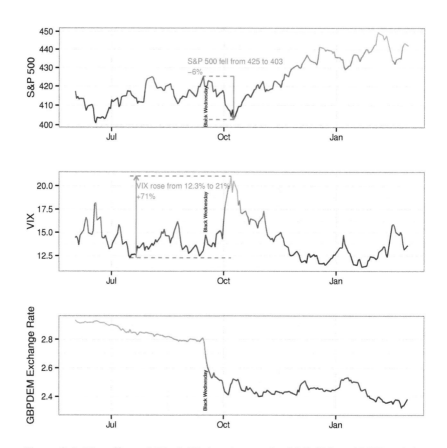

Figure 2.4: The effect of Black Wednesday on the S&P 500 and VIX and the sterling to Deutsche Mark exchange rate. Source: Bloomberg.

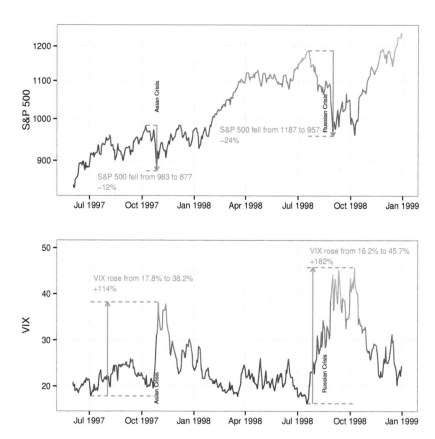

Figure 2.6: The effect of the Asian and Russian crises on the S&P 500 and VIX. Source: Bloomberg.

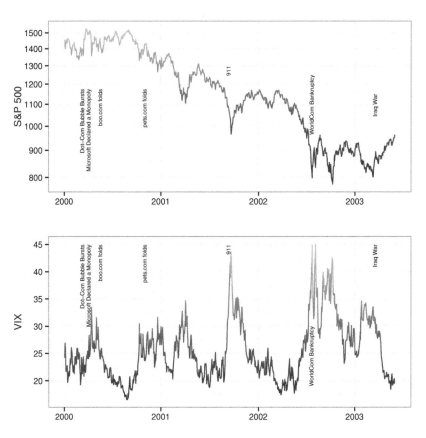

Figure 2.7: The effect of the Dot-Com bubble, 9/11, WorldCom bankruptcy and Iraq War on the S&P 500 and VIX. Source: Bloomberg.

The Credit Crisis

If you had perfect foresight the ideal would be to buy volatility just before each crisis and sell just as the crisis peaked. November 2008 marked the peak for VIX, and this would have been the time to close your volatility position (Figure 2.8). Up until the beginning of September 2008 there was no sign of trouble reflected in the volatility market, because VIX was still around its long-term average of 20%. After the Lehman default on September 15th VIX jumped above 30% and carried on rising. The dragon was awake. However the S&P 500 share index took another month to fall sharply below 1000. Critically this means that you would have had time to buy volatility before it peaked at just over 80% in November. Chapter 4 lists some rules of thumb to help guide you when to buy and sell volatility.

Volatility is driven by shocks, and these usually come from headlines in the media. If you want to get a feel for the kind of news that drives volatility higher and lower, the period between August 2007 and February 2009 are very instructive. The big players were the investment banks and the US central bank, the Federal Reserve. When the Fed senses trouble in financial markets it cuts its Fed Funds Target Rate. The theory is that this reduces interest rates and makes credit more readily available for individuals and businesses. This in turn increases disposable income and spending on consumer goods and services, creates greater corporate profits and stimulates the economy.

The equity market often gets a boost when the Fed cuts rates, and a rising equity market usually drives volatility lower. However Fed rate cuts send a double signal. They show, in the short term, that the Fed is willing to act to prop up the economy which is in serious trouble. Volatility investors stand to make money when a crisis occurs and so for them a Fed rate cut is good news in the short term while the crisis lasts but bad news if the rate cut successfully brings about an equity rally.

On August 17, 2007, the Federal Reserve cut rates from 6.25% to 5.75% citing fears that the Credit Crisis could be a risk to economic growth. Volatility, as measured by the VIX index, had risen to 30%, but as a result of the Fed's rate policy, markets were reassured, equities rallied and VIX fell back down to its long-term average of 20% over the following months. The Fed cut rates again to 4.75% on September 18th and this stimulated markets again. At the same time the rate at which banks lend to one another, the LIBOR rate, started to soar. Banks were concerned about one another's exposure to sub-prime assets, and this made lending more risky, so they demanded a higher rate. Then the losses from sub-prime mortgages began to emerge. On October

1st 2007 UBS announced losses of $3.4 billion due to sub-prime exposure and the chairman and chief executive resigned. Citigroup later announced losses of $5.9 billion, and on October 30th Merrill Lynch announced losses of $7.9 billion and, again, the chief executive resigned. All this bad news rattled markets. Equity markets started their long decline with these loss announcements. As equities fell, volatility rose up to 30% again.

The steep decline in equities in 2007 and the beginning of 2008 led the Fed to make its biggest rate cut in 25 years on January 22nd 2008. The Fed cut rates from 4.25% to 3.5%. This was enough to stabilize equity markets for the next four months, and volatility fell to its resting state of 20% once more. Bad headlines soon re-emerged as further losses were announced and banks tried to shore up their balance sheets by issuing more shares. The double-shock that finally brought the crisis to a head was the announcement on September 7th that Fannie Mae and Freddie Mac, two companies that were created to help guarantee mortgages and boost the housing market, were being nationalized.[3] This was followed by the bankruptcy of Lehman Brothers just a week later on September 15th. After this double-blow VIX soared rapidly to new record levels, peaking on November 20th at 80.86% (see Figure 2.9). Interestingly VIX did not react immediately remaining below 40% for a few weeks following the Lehman default (see Figure 2.9). Then a very large savings bank called Washington Mutual became bankrupt on September 25th.

The Fed did all that it could using its interest rate policy, but this was not enough to avoid a catastrophic fall in equity markets. Stronger medicine was required, and so the Fed started to adopt unconventional policy measures. With conventional policy the Fed sets short-term interest rates. Longer-term interest rates, which affect rates for longer-term loans, can remain stubbornly high. By buying US government bonds the Fed pushed up their prices and this pushed down the interest they paid. The overall aim was to push down long-term interest rates and make longer-term borrowing cheaper. This unconventional policy is called quantitative easing. Central bank policy is easy to monitor because it always hits the headlines. When volatility investors see "Fed rate cut" or "Fed policy easing", they would expect the equity market to rise and volatility to fall. When they see "Fed rate hike" or "Fed policy tightening", equity markets tend to fall and volatility may rise if there is a sudden or unexpected hike.

---

[3]In the US the word "conservatorship" is preferred to "nationalized".

The Fed's Solution: Quantitative Easing

As usual the Fed used conventional monetary policy to help boost economic growth (and indirectly the stock market) by reducing borrowing rates for individuals and companies. For a crisis of this scale this medicine was too weak to deal with the aftermath of the collapse of Lehman in September 2008. Unconventional policy proved more effective, as the Fed launched three rounds of quantitative easing (QE), the third of which involved continual buying of $85 billion a month in Treasuries and Mortgage Backed Securities (see Figure 2.10). Between QE2 and QE3 was Operation Twist which bought more long-term Treasuries and less short-term Treasuries in order to reduce long-term interest rates.

During the period of recession from December 2007 until June 2009 unemployment surged to over 10% and there was a brief period of deflation. Fed Chairman Bernanke saw deflation as a serious threat to the US economy and some even thought that the US would see long-term deflation and low-growth as had happened in Japan for decades. However the Federal Reserve's QE1 combined with the government's Troubled Asset Relief Program succeeded in ending deflation before the end of 2009. Unemployment, however, remained stubbornly high even as stocks rallied strongly and volatility fell. At the time of writing QE3 is ongoing but the Federal reserve says that once unemployment reaches 6.5% it will start tapering its asset purchases.

From the point of view of a volatility investor quantitative easing was decreasingly important each time it was used. Removal of QE3 is interesting because the Fed is removing the backstop for the US economy. Some people believe that stock prices are artificially inflated by low interest rates. If this reasoning is correct it may drive a pick-up in volatility as a result as stock prices fall. The argument against an equity bubble is that the reason for removing QE is that the economy is growing and moving away from deflation with very low inflation. Historically this is a recipe for good stock performance and low volatility. This would be an environment to sell volatility (for example see the strategy in the section "Strategy 2: Long/Short Short-term VIX Futures" in Chapter 4).

The US government's solution: TARP

The US government created the Troubled Asset Relief Program (TARP). This was a fund of colossal size, initially containing $700 billion in October 2008, almost all of which was recovered over the next five years.[4] TARP was used to do the following:

Bail Out Banks $250 billion of TARP was used to stabilize the banking system following the default of Lehman. There were five bank bailout programs and the largest was the Capital Purchase Program which invested $205 billion in 707 institutions including 450 small and community banks. In addition to their CPP investments investment banks were helped by the Targeted Investment Program which provided $20 billion to Bank of America and $20 billion to Citigroup. The TIP program was closed by December 2009 with a profit of $4 billion.

Bail Out the Automobile Industry The crisis made it much harder to get car loans, and job insecurity as companies shrank their workforce made people much less likely to commit to larger purchases such as new cars. The automotive industry was an early casualty and $82 billion of TARP was used to help ailing manufacturers through the crisis. The companies bailed out were Chrysler ($12.4 billion), GM ($50 billion) and Ally Financial ($17.2 billion). Out of a total $80 billion provided to the auto industry it is estimated that $20 billion will not be recovered, but the companies were helped to restructure through orderly bankruptcy, were returned to profitability and created a quarter of a million new jobs from June 2009 to 2013.

Bail Out AIG AIG is a multinational US insurance company that amassed a large portfolio of credit default swaps that lost money as credit risk increased. This threatened to make AIG insolvent. Given the links of AIG to many other companies and individuals this was considered to be unacceptable and $182 billion of TARP was used to bail out AIG. This was fully recovered with an additional $22.7 billion profit when the fund sold its stake.

Bail Out Households $46 billion of TARP was used to help families who had bought homes they could not afford to avoid foreclosure. This carried a lot of political capital because it helped American families avoid being forced out of their homes if they could not make their mortgage repayments.

Bail Out the Credit Market The flow of credit is pivotal in the US economy to finance businesses and consumers, so $27 billion was used to

---

[4]See http://www.treasury.gov/initiatives/financial-stability.

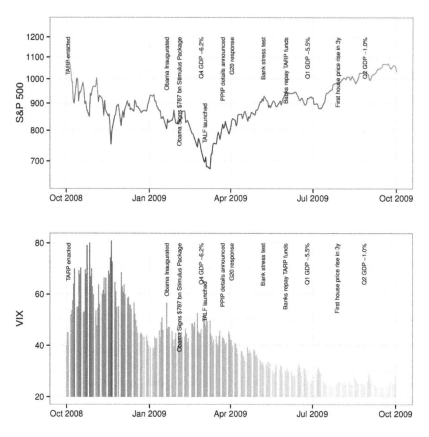

Figure 2.11: Resolution of the Credit Crisis. Source: Bloomberg.

Standard & Poor's	Fitch	Moody's	p(Default in 5Y)	Quality
		Investment Grade		
AAA	AAA	Aaa	0.06%	Highest quality
AA+	AA+	Aa1	0.10%	
AA	AA	Aa2	0.22%	High quality
AA-	AA-	Aa3	0.28%	
A+	A+	A1	0.37%	
A	A	A2	0.46%	Upper Medium Grade
A-	A-	A3	0.69%	
BBB+	BBB+	Baa1	1.39%	
BBB	BBB	Baa2	2.32%	Medium Grade
BBB-	BBB-	Baa3	5.18%	
		Sub Investment Grade		
BB+	BB+	Ba1	7.02%	
BB	BB	Ba2	10.42%	Lower Medium Grade
BB-	BB-	Ba3	14.60%	
B+	B+	B1	18.57%	
B	B	B2	24.46%	Low Grade
B-	B-	B3	34.33%	
CCC+	CCC+	Caa1	55.81%	
CCC	CCC	Caa2	70.04%	Poor Quality
CCC-	CCC-	Caa3	85.51%	
CC	CC	Ca	100%	Very poor quality
C	C	C	100%	Bankruptcy filed
D	D			In default

Table 2.1: Long-term credit rating codes and probability of default within five years. Source: Bloomberg, S&P.

predicted an extended period of subdued economic growth which would weaken Spain's budgetary position.

May 2010 Greek Bailout A three-year Greek bailout deal worth 110 billion euros was organized by the ECB on May 2nd, European Commission and International Monetary Fund. In return Greece had to agree to cut its spending dramatically.

May 2010 Flash Crash Sometimes markets tumble because of a spiral of fear which feeds upon itself. On May 6th 2010 the Dow Jones suffered a spectacular drop of 9% in one day. After a lengthy investigation it turned out that the trigger for the crash was a large fund manager selling a substantial number of S&P 500 futures (called E-Mini futures). Computer trading algorithms almost instantaneously spotted the large number of sell orders and pounced rapidly. High frequency traders tried to make money by shorting the E-Mini and profiting from the fall. Their algorithms did so by selling more E-Mini contracts, driving the price down further and faster in a self-perpetuating spiral. The entire drama played out in seconds. At 2:45:28pm, trading on the Chicago Mercantile Exchange was automatically suspended for five seconds to give the market a breather. It worked. Buyers emerged and the tumble was stopped. By 2:45:33 pm prices started to bottom out and the E-Mini and the S&P 500 began to recover.

May 2010 Spain Rating Cut Fitch cut its sovereign debt rating for Spain by one notch from AAA to AA+ on May 28th on expectations that the moves to cut the nation's debt would slow its economic growth. This announcement came one day after Spain had announced new austerity measures to cut its budget deficit.

July 2010 Ireland Rating Cut Moody's cut Ireland's rating from Aa1 to Aa2 on July 19th.

August 2010 Ireland Rating Cut On August 24th S&P downgraded Ireland from AA to AA- citing the cost to the Irish government of supporting the Irish financial sector.

September 2010 Spain Rating Cut Moody's cut Spain's Aaa rating to Aa1 because of weak economic growth prospects relative to other top-rated countries, and the extended period of time it would take to rebalance the economy away from the construction and real-estate sectors. Moody's

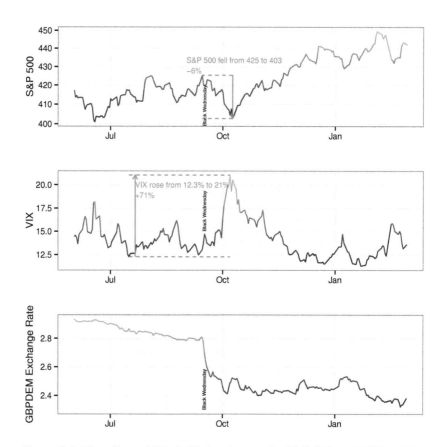

Figure 2.4: The effect of Black Wednesday on the S&P 500 and VIX and the sterling to Deutsche Mark exchange rate. Source: Bloomberg.

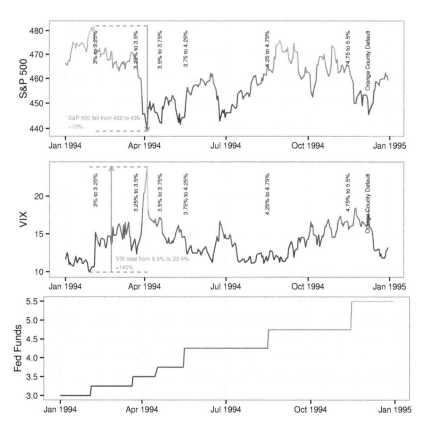

Figure 2.5: The effect of Fed interest rate rises on the S&P 500 and VIX. Source: Bloomberg.

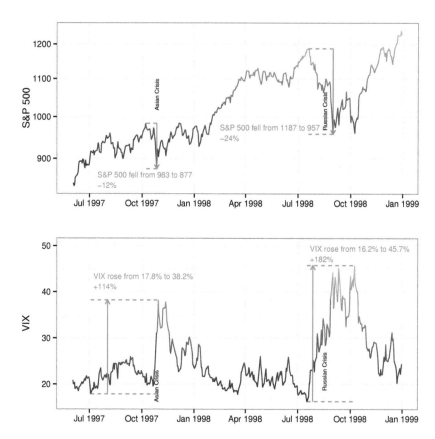

Figure 2.6: The effect of the Asian and Russian crises on the S&P 500 and VIX. Source: Bloomberg.

before the default, on July 17th VIX surged from 16% to levels around 30%. The Russian debt default pushed VIX up further to levels around 40% where it stayed until October 8th when the Fed cut interest rates to boost stock markets. After the rate cut the US stock market recovered and volatility fell.

2000 DotCom *Dot-Com Bubble Burst* No single event marks the demise of the dot-com bubble but the turn-around point when share prices stopped increasing was around March 2000. The value of a share can be measured by dividing its share price by how much money each share earns each year. This is called the price to earnings ratio, often abbreviated to P/E ratio. Typically the price of a share ranges from 10 times its earnings to 30 times its earnings with the upper end reserved for stocks that have a strong prospect of increasing their earnings in future by growth or acquisitions. During the dot-com boom companies that had no earnings at all, or had negative earnings as they burned seed capital, had P/E ratios that were hugely over-inflated, often above 50. As sanity returned prices tumbled back to more realistic P/E levels, new stock listings for dot-coms dried up and a spate of bankruptcies followed. The effect was a long and sustained surge in volatility.

2001 911 *Nine Eleven* The terrorist attack on the US resulting in the destruction of the Twin Towers and the World Trade Center in New York was a massive shock to global markets, particularly those in the US. Equity markets were closed directly after the attacks because many investment banks had offices in the Twin Towers, but predictably when markets re-opened shares sold off and VIX surged to just under 45%.

2002 WorldCom *WorldCom Bankruptcy* The CEO of WorldCom had a sizeable stake in his own company's shares and in collaboration with several other senior managers of the company used fraudulent accounting practices to overstate the assets of the company. The fraud was perpetrated to boost the WorldCom share price and the personal wealth of the conspirators. The US Securities and Exchange Commission started an investigation into WorldCom's accounts on June 26, 2002. On July 21st 2002 WorldCom filed for bankruptcy, the largest bankruptcy in US corporate history up to that point in time.

2003 IraqWar *Iraq War* A coalition of countries invaded Iraq in order to topple the dictator Saddam Hussein and to rid Iraq of weapons of mass

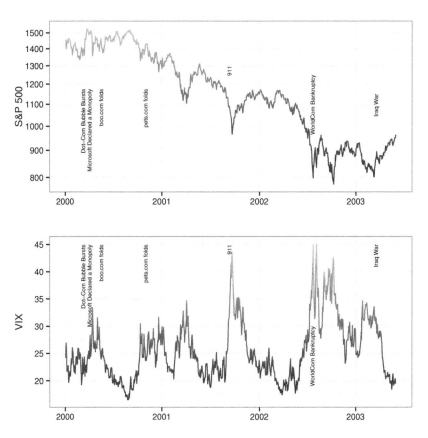

Figure 2.7: The effect of the Dot-Com bubble, 9/11, WorldCom bankruptcy and Iraq War on the S&P 500 and VIX. Source: Bloomberg.

destruction. Military operations started on March 19th 2003 and lasted until May 1st and ended with the capture of Baghdad in April. Although no weapons of mass destruction were discovered the US stock market rallied strongly during and after the war. In this case war restored confidence and lowered VIX from 30% to 20%.

2003-2007 Volatility Crash The period from September 2003 to July 2007 was one of very low volatility. This was due to the strong equity rally during this quiet four-year period of growth. There was just one volatility blip as the Fed hiked interest rates in 2006.

2004 FedRtShock2 *Fed Rate Hike* Alan Greenspan had been Chairman of the Federal Reserve for eighteen years, and his successor Ben Bernanke was sworn in on January 31st 2006. Alan Greenspan had started hiking rates on June 30th 2004 from a starting level of 1% and rising at a rate of about 2 percentage points per year. Bernanke continued the trend until June 2006.

2006 WeakDollar *Weakening Dollar* Worries about the size of the US fiscal deficit due to the cost of tax cuts and the war in Iraq combined with a widening trade deficit made the US dollar weaken sharply. Stock markets sold off in sympathy as the worries bled from the foreign exchange market to the equity market, and VIX doubled from 12% in May to peak at 24% in June. This brief spike in VIX stands out during the ultra-low volatility of the 2003-2007 volatility crash.

2007 BNPHdgFnd *BNP Paribas Closes Three Sub-prime Hedge Funds* On August 9th 2007 the French investment bank shocked markets when it closed three funds with a combined value of €1.6 billion: Parvest Dynamic ABS, BNP Paribas ABS Euribor and BNP Paribas ABS Eonia. The bank justified its action by stating that there was a "complete evaporation of liquidity in certain market segments of the US securitisation market". The asset backed securities owned by the funds contained sub-prime loans in the US housing market and this was one of the first warning signs that the sub-prime market was about to implode. This news was greeted with a fall in share prices and a rise in VIX.

The Credit Crisis

If you had perfect foresight the ideal would be to buy volatility just before each crisis and sell just as the crisis peaked. November 2008 marked the peak for VIX, and this would have been the time to close your volatility position (Figure 2.8). Up until the beginning of September 2008 there was no sign of trouble reflected in the volatility market, because VIX was still around its long-term average of 20%. After the Lehman default on September 15th VIX jumped above 30% and carried on rising. The dragon was awake. However the S&P 500 share index took another month to fall sharply below 1000. Critically this means that you would have had time to buy volatility before it peaked at just over 80% in November. Chapter 4 lists some rules of thumb to help guide you when to buy and sell volatility.

Volatility is driven by shocks, and these usually come from headlines in the media. If you want to get a feel for the kind of news that drives volatility higher and lower, the period between August 2007 and February 2009 are very instructive. The big players were the investment banks and the US central bank, the Federal Reserve. When the Fed senses trouble in financial markets it cuts its Fed Funds Target Rate. The theory is that this reduces interest rates and makes credit more readily available for individuals and businesses. This in turn increases disposable income and spending on consumer goods and services, creates greater corporate profits and stimulates the economy.

The equity market often gets a boost when the Fed cuts rates, and a rising equity market usually drives volatility lower. However Fed rate cuts send a double signal. They show, in the short term, that the Fed is willing to act to prop up the economy which is in serious trouble. Volatility investors stand to make money when a crisis occurs and so for them a Fed rate cut is good news in the short term while the crisis lasts but bad news if the rate cut successfully brings about an equity rally.

On August 17, 2007, the Federal Reserve cut rates from 6.25% to 5.75% citing fears that the Credit Crisis could be a risk to economic growth. Volatility, as measured by the VIX index, had risen to 30%, but as a result of the Fed's rate policy, markets were reassured, equities rallied and VIX fell back down to its long-term average of 20% over the following months. The Fed cut rates again to 4.75% on September 18th and this stimulated markets again. At the same time the rate at which banks lend to one another, the LIBOR rate, started to soar. Banks were concerned about one another's exposure to sub-prime assets, and this made lending more risky, so they demanded a higher rate. Then the losses from sub-prime mortgages began to emerge. On October

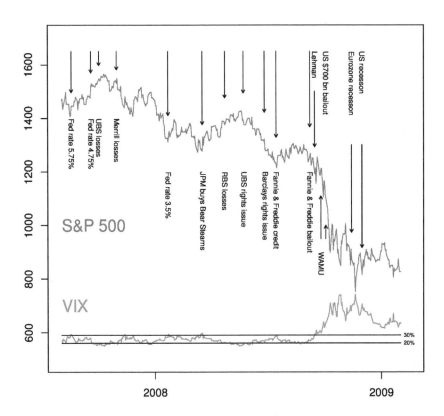

Figure 2.8: S&P 500 share index and VIX volatility index leading up to the Lehman Brothers and WAMU defaults. Source: Bloomberg.

1st 2007 UBS announced losses of $3.4 billion due to sub-prime exposure and the chairman and chief executive resigned. Citigroup later announced losses of $5.9 billion, and on October 30th Merrill Lynch announced losses of $7.9 billion and, again, the chief executive resigned. All this bad news rattled markets. Equity markets started their long decline with these loss announcements. As equities fell, volatility rose up to 30% again.

The steep decline in equities in 2007 and the beginning of 2008 led the Fed to make its biggest rate cut in 25 years on January 22nd 2008. The Fed cut rates from 4.25% to 3.5%. This was enough to stabilize equity markets for the next four months, and volatility fell to its resting state of 20% once more. Bad headlines soon re-emerged as further losses were announced and banks tried to shore up their balance sheets by issuing more shares. The double-shock that finally brought the crisis to a head was the announcement on September 7th that Fannie Mae and Freddie Mac, two companies that were created to help guarantee mortgages and boost the housing market, were being nationalized.[3] This was followed by the bankruptcy of Lehman Brothers just a week later on September 15th. After this double-blow VIX soared rapidly to new record levels, peaking on November 20th at 80.86% (see Figure 2.9). Interestingly VIX did not react immediately remaining below 40% for a few weeks following the Lehman default (see Figure 2.9). Then a very large savings bank called Washington Mutual became bankrupt on September 25th.

The Fed did all that it could using its interest rate policy, but this was not enough to avoid a catastrophic fall in equity markets. Stronger medicine was required, and so the Fed started to adopt unconventional policy measures. With conventional policy the Fed sets short-term interest rates. Longer-term interest rates, which affect rates for longer-term loans, can remain stubbornly high. By buying US government bonds the Fed pushed up their prices and this pushed down the interest they paid. The overall aim was to push down long-term interest rates and make longer-term borrowing cheaper. This unconventional policy is called quantitative easing. Central bank policy is easy to monitor because it always hits the headlines. When volatility investors see "Fed rate cut" or "Fed policy easing", they would expect the equity market to rise and volatility to fall. When they see "Fed rate hike" or "Fed policy tightening", equity markets tend to fall and volatility may rise if there is a sudden or unexpected hike.

---

[3]In the US the word "conservatorship" is preferred to "nationalized".

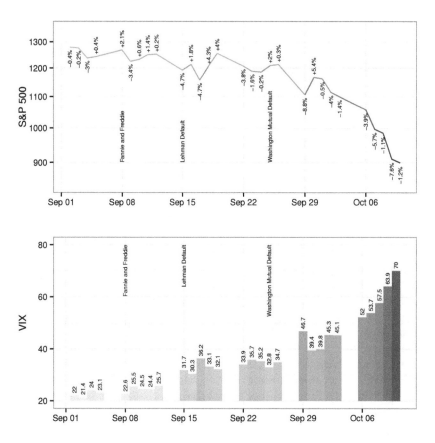

Figure 2.9: Volatility increased above 30% in 2008 well before the S&P 500 fell sharply. Source: Bloomberg.

The Fed's Solution: Quantitative Easing

As usual the Fed used conventional monetary policy to help boost economic growth (and indirectly the stock market) by reducing borrowing rates for individuals and companies. For a crisis of this scale this medicine was too weak to deal with the aftermath of the collapse of Lehman in September 2008. Unconventional policy proved more effective, as the Fed launched three rounds of quantitative easing (QE), the third of which involved continual buying of $85 billion a month in Treasuries and Mortgage Backed Securities (see Figure 2.10). Between QE2 and QE3 was Operation Twist which bought more long-term Treasuries and less short-term Treasuries in order to reduce long-term interest rates.

During the period of recession from December 2007 until June 2009 unemployment surged to over 10% and there was a brief period of deflation. Fed Chairman Bernanke saw deflation as a serious threat to the US economy and some even thought that the US would see long-term deflation and low-growth as had happened in Japan for decades. However the Federal Reserve's QE1 combined with the government's Troubled Asset Relief Program succeeded in ending deflation before the end of 2009. Unemployment, however, remained stubbornly high even as stocks rallied strongly and volatility fell. At the time of writing QE3 is ongoing but the Federal reserve says that once unemployment reaches 6.5% it will start tapering its asset purchases.

From the point of view of a volatility investor quantitative easing was decreasingly important each time it was used. Removal of QE3 is interesting because the Fed is removing the backstop for the US economy. Some people believe that stock prices are artificially inflated by low interest rates. If this reasoning is correct it may drive a pick-up in volatility as a result as stock prices fall. The argument against an equity bubble is that the reason for removing QE is that the economy is growing and moving away from deflation with very low inflation. Historically this is a recipe for good stock performance and low volatility. This would be an environment to sell volatility (for example see the strategy in the section "Strategy 2: Long/Short Short-term VIX Futures" in Chapter 4).

The US government's solution: TARP

The US government created the Troubled Asset Relief Program (TARP). This was a fund of colossal size, initially containing $700 billion in October 2008,

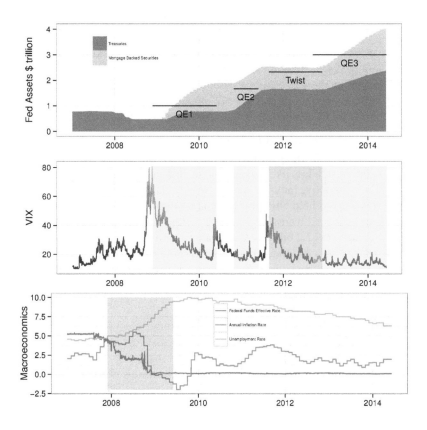

Figure 2.10: The effects of the Federal Reserve's unconventional monetary policy (quantitative easing or QE). Blue shaded region marks US recession, yellow shaded region denotes periods of QE, green shaded region is Operation Twist. Source: Bloomberg. and Federal Reserve Bank of St. Louis.

almost all of which was recovered over the next five years.[4] TARP was used to do the following:

Bail Out Banks $250 billion of TARP was used to stabilize the banking system following the default of Lehman. There were five bank bailout programs and the largest was the Capital Purchase Program which invested $205 billion in 707 institutions including 450 small and community banks. In addition to their CPP investments investment banks were helped by the Targeted Investment Program which provided $20 billion to Bank of America and $20 billion to Citigroup. The TIP program was closed by December 2009 with a profit of $4 billion.

Bail Out the Automobile Industry The crisis made it much harder to get car loans, and job insecurity as companies shrank their workforce made people much less likely to commit to larger purchases such as new cars. The automotive industry was an early casualty and $82 billion of TARP was used to help ailing manufacturers through the crisis. The companies bailed out were Chrysler ($12.4 billion), GM ($50 billion) and Ally Financial ($17.2 billion). Out of a total $80 billion provided to the auto industry it is estimated that $20 billion will not be recovered, but the companies were helped to restructure through orderly bankruptcy, were returned to profitability and created a quarter of a million new jobs from June 2009 to 2013.

Bail Out AIG AIG is a multinational US insurance company that amassed a large portfolio of credit default swaps that lost money as credit risk increased. This threatened to make AIG insolvent. Given the links of AIG to many other companies and individuals this was considered to be unacceptable and $182 billion of TARP was used to bail out AIG. This was fully recovered with an additional $22.7 billion profit when the fund sold its stake.

Bail Out Households $46 billion of TARP was used to help families who had bought homes they could not afford to avoid foreclosure. This carried a lot of political capital because it helped American families avoid being forced out of their homes if they could not make their mortgage repayments.

Bail Out the Credit Market The flow of credit is pivotal in the US economy to finance businesses and consumers, so $27 billion was used to

---

[4]See http://www.treasury.gov/initiatives/financial-stability.

keep this market going. This was split into the Term Asset Loan Facility (TALF) which pledged $20 billion and helped create 3 million auto loans, 1 million student loans 900,000 small business loans and millions of credit card loans. $18.6 billion was invested in the Legacy Securities Public-Private Investment Program (PPIP) which provided loans to help private investors buy crisis-battered mortgage-related products from banks, insurance companies, mutual funds, and pension funds.

The turning point for stock prices and the inflection point for volatility to fall below its 40% to 50% trading band in Q1 2009 was around March 2009. It is probably not a coincidence that the inflection occurred at the same as the creation of the Term Asset Loan Facility which successfully unfroze the loan market. However it is impossible to separate the positive effects of ongoing quantitative easing by the Fed, and it was probably a combination of QE, TARP, and improving corporate earnings that eased investor fears and drove volatility lower.

The European Sovereign Debt Crisis

Following the creation of the single European currency — the euro — in 1999, member states could issue their own government bonds denominated in euro. Government bonds allow a sovereign to top up its income, and the rate of interest that they pay depends on how sought-after their bonds are. A government that has a recent history of not repaying its debt, such as Argentina, will have to pay a higher level of interest to lure investors to take its credit risk.

Figure 2.12 shows the cost of borrowing for five European countries from 2000 to 2013. For the decade beginning with the formation of the euro and ending with the Credit Crisis in 2009 the European government bond market treated all bonds the same, demanding similar rates of interest whether they were issued in Greece, Portugal, Ireland or Germany. This led to some "peripheral" economies such as Portugal, Ireland, Greece and, to a lesser extent, Spain, gorging on cheap funding which they were unable to repay. Cheap money also fueled housing bubbles in Ireland, Spain and the UK.

After the Credit Crisis started to wane in 2009 markets woke up to the fact that some sovereigns would struggle to pay back their lenders as a worldwide recession started to lower their tax revenue. Markets punished the peripheral bond markets by selling their bonds. This meant the peripheral countries had to offer higher rates of interest to make their bonds attractive to investors making

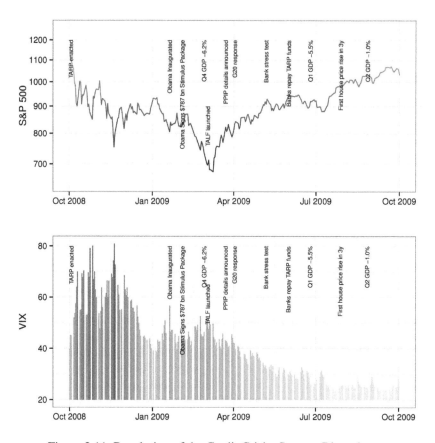

Figure 2.11: Resolution of the Credit Crisis. Source: Bloomberg.

their debt repayments even more costly. Core countries such as Germany, the Netherlands, France, Belgium and Finland saw a sharp reduction in their bond yield as investors flocked to their relative safety. The crisis led to a default by Greece and a series of banking bailouts as homeowners defaulted on their mortgages. This caused global repercussions in the equity market, driving share prices lower and increasing volatility world-wide.

The credit ratings agencies played a large part in the European sovereign debt crisis, so it may help to know a little bit about credit ratings and the companies that create them. The three biggest are Standard and Poor's, Moody's and Fitch. Table 2.1 shows the ratings agencies and their classifications. The key difference is investment grade and sub investment grade (known rather unkindly as junk) which occurs as the rating falls below BBB for Standard and Poor's and below Baa for Moody's. Many bond investors have a mandate not to buy sub investment grade bonds because they carry too much risk of default. Consequently when a company, or a country, is judged to have a junk credit rating there is a rush to sell their bonds and their borrowing costs may surge. This occurred when Greece was downgraded to junk by S&P in April 2010. Ratings come with approximate default probabilities. For a AAA credit the risk of them not repaying their bonds is almost zero. For BB credits, which is the highest junk rating, the risk of defaulting within five years is about 10%.

January 2009 Greece Downgraded by S&P As one of the first signs of trouble, the ratings agency Standard and Poors downgraded Greece by one notch from A to A- on January 14th, citing concerns about entering an economic downturn with a high government deficit and gross debt estimated at 94.1% of GDP in 2008. Greece had repeatedly failed to stick to budgetary plans with "regular deficit-increasing one-offs and expenditure slippages". This concerned S&P which saw this as weak fiscal management.

April 2010 Greece Downgraded to Junk by S&P As it became clear that Greece would not be able to repay its bonds, S&P downgraded its credit rating to junk bond status (from BB+ to BBB+) on April 27th citing an updated assessment of the political, economic, and budgetary challenges that the Greek government faced in its efforts to put the public debt burden onto a sustained downward trajectory. As a result of the downgrade the cost of ten-year Greek borrowing jumped up by around 2% to 9.8%. At the same time S&P downgraded Portugal by two-notches from A+ to A-. The next day it cut Spain's rating from AAA to AA because it

Standard & Poor's	Fitch	Moody's	p(Default in 5Y)	Quality
Investment Grade				
AAA	AAA	Aaa	0.06%	Highest quality
AA+	AA+	Aa1	0.10%	
AA	AA	Aa2	0.22%	High quality
AA-	AA-	Aa3	0.28%	
A+	A+	A1	0.37%	
A	A	A2	0.46%	Upper Medium Grade
A-	A-	A3	0.69%	
BBB+	BBB+	Baa1	1.39%	
BBB	BBB	Baa2	2.32%	Medium Grade
BBB-	BBB-	Baa3	5.18%	
Sub Investment Grade				
BB+	BB+	Ba1	7.02%	
BB	BB	Ba2	10.42%	Lower Medium Grade
BB-	BB-	Ba3	14.60%	
B+	B+	B1	18.57%	
B	B	B2	24.46%	Low Grade
B-	B-	B3	34.33%	
CCC+	CCC+	Caa1	55.81%	
CCC	CCC	Caa2	70.04%	Poor Quality
CCC-	CCC-	Caa3	85.51%	
CC	CC	Ca	100%	Very poor quality
C	C	C	100%	Bankruptcy filed
D	D			In default

Table 2.1: Long-term credit rating codes and probability of default within five years. Source: Bloomberg, S&P.

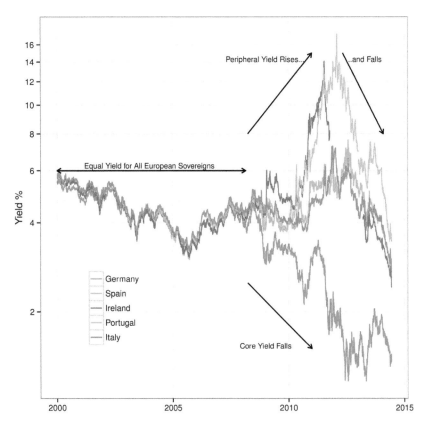

Figure 2.12: Cost of ten year borrowing for European sovereigns. Source: Bloomberg.

predicted an extended period of subdued economic growth which would weaken Spain's budgetary position.

May 2010 Greek Bailout A three-year Greek bailout deal worth 110 billion euros was organized by the ECB on May 2nd, European Commission and International Monetary Fund. In return Greece had to agree to cut its spending dramatically.

May 2010 Flash Crash Sometimes markets tumble because of a spiral of fear which feeds upon itself. On May 6th 2010 the Dow Jones suffered a spectacular drop of 9% in one day. After a lengthy investigation it turned out that the trigger for the crash was a large fund manager selling a substantial number of S&P 500 futures (called E-Mini futures). Computer trading algorithms almost instantaneously spotted the large number of sell orders and pounced rapidly. High frequency traders tried to make money by shorting the E-Mini and profiting from the fall. Their algorithms did so by selling more E-Mini contracts, driving the price down further and faster in a self-perpetuating spiral. The entire drama played out in seconds. At 2:45:28pm, trading on the Chicago Mercantile Exchange was automatically suspended for five seconds to give the market a breather. It worked. Buyers emerged and the tumble was stopped. By 2:45:33 pm prices started to bottom out and the E-Mini and the S&P 500 began to recover.

May 2010 Spain Rating Cut Fitch cut its sovereign debt rating for Spain by one notch from AAA to AA+ on May 28th on expectations that the moves to cut the nation's debt would slow its economic growth. This announcement came one day after Spain had announced new austerity measures to cut its budget deficit.

July 2010 Ireland Rating Cut Moody's cut Ireland's rating from Aa1 to Aa2 on July 19th.

August 2010 Ireland Rating Cut On August 24th S&P downgraded Ireland from AA to AA- citing the cost to the Irish government of supporting the Irish financial sector.

September 2010 Spain Rating Cut Moody's cut Spain's Aaa rating to Aa1 because of weak economic growth prospects relative to other top-rated countries, and the extended period of time it would take to rebalance the economy away from the construction and real-estate sectors. Moody's also pointed out that the Spanish government's financial strength was waning and the cost of its interest payments as a share of revenue was rising.

November 2010 Irish Bailout On November 28th the European Union, International Monetary Fund and UK, Denmark and Sweden provided €67.5 billion of loans to the Irish government and Irish banks. A further €17.5 billion came from Irish national reserves and pensions.

March 2011 Tohoku Earthquake and Tsunami On March 11th there was a massive offshore earthquake that generated a large tsunami which devastated the east coast of Japan. Subsequently nuclear reactors at Fukushima suffered a meltdown as their cooling pumps failed. A state of emergency was declared and 480,000 people living within 20 km of the nuclear plant had to be evacuated. The disruption to power supplies in Japan was severe, and the economic impacts to supply chains were global in nature. Once the nuclear meltdown occurred volatility rose sharply in the US equity market, but the spike was short-lived.

May 2011 Portugal Bailout The European Union and International Monetary Fund (IMF) agreed to provide €78 billion in loans to Portugal on May 17th. The condition for this aid was that Portugal should cut its 2011 deficit from 9.1% to 5.9%.

August 2011 US Debt Ceiling The US government gets income from taxes and spends money on health care, social security, defense and infrastructure. Any gap between the two is topped up with debt issued by the US Treasury. However since 1917 US law has set a cap on the amount of debt the Treasury can issue and Congress has to approve raising this cap, or debt ceiling. Unfortunately Democrats and Republicans disagree fundamentally on how to balance the books: Republicans want to cut spending, usually on health and social security, whereas Democrats want to reduce spending on the military and increase income by raising taxes. In 1979 the US had come to the brink of a default as Republicans tried to stop Democratic President Jimmy Carter from raising the ceiling. Echoing that event in 2011 Republicans tried to stop Democratic President Barack Obama from raising the debt ceiling. The rating agency S&P downgraded the US from AAA to AA+ on August 5th 2011, and although this did not push Treasury yields up the combination of a downgrade and last-minute negotiations did push stock markets down by 20% and tripled volatility from 16% to 48% (see Figure 3.2).

November 2011 Swap Lines During the European Sovereign Debt Crisis it was difficult for European banks to pay their US liabilities because they needed loans in dollars to service those debts. US banks were not keen to provide dollar loans to European banks which were known to be in crisis. Also few US customers wanted to put their dollar deposits in European banks. Central banks therefore agreed swap lines whereby the Fed would swap dollars with the currency of the other central banks (notably euro for the ECB) and would also provide dollar loans to those banks. The ECB could then provide these dollars and dollar loans to its regional banks to ease their dollar funding problems. As a result of the European sovereign crisis these joint central bank liquidity agreements that had previously been put in place during the Credit Crisis were extended until February 2013.

March 2012 Greek Default In March 2012 Greece's debt burden had reached 160% of its gross domestic product. The Troika, consisting of the European Commission, ECB and IMF, insisted that it reduce its debt burden to around 120% of gross domestic product as a pre-condition of receiving a package of €130 billion in bailout loans. The Greek government decided the best way to reduce their debt was a debt swap whereby private sector investors would agree to swap their Greek bonds for new ones which were worth less. The reduction in value is called a haircut. Greece had issued €177 billion in bonds under Greek law of which bond holders of €152 billion agreed to receive a 74% haircut. Because some investors were forced to accept a haircut involuntarily this was defined as a default.

June 2012 Spain Rating Cut Moody's rating agency cut Spain's government bonds by three notches from A3 to Baa3. This was just one notch above junk status. The Spanish bond market is much larger than that of Greece and a downgrade to junk would have had much larger repercussions as many pension funds and asset managers are not allowed to invest in junk bonds. A downgrade to junk would have caused forced selling by these investors and would have sharply increased Spanish yields.

June 2012 Spanish Bank Bailout Spain's problem was quite unlike that of Greece where the government had borrowed too much. Instead the problem lay with Spanish banks which saw many of their property loans go into arrears or default when the housing bubble burst. For example Bankia, which was created in a merger between seven regional savings

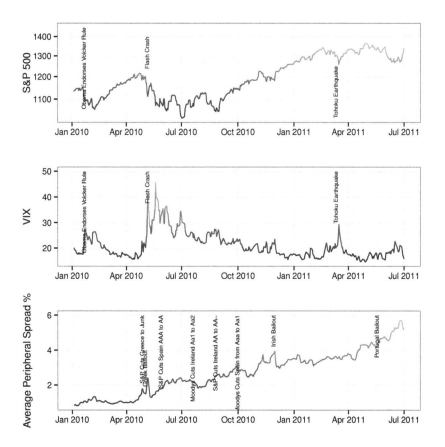

Figure 2.13: The effect of the Flash Crash, Tohoku earthquake and European sovereign debt crisis on the S&P 500 and VIX. Source: Bloomberg.

banks, said in June 2012 that it had a capital shortfall of €19 billion. In June Spain requested aid for its banks from eurozone finance ministers who agreed a €100 billion bailout package which targeted Spanish banks through the Fund for Orderly Bank Restructuring (FROB). The call for aid came less than 24 hours after the publication of an IMF report on the Spanish banking sector that described the banking crisis as being "unprecedented in its modern history".

July 2012 Whatever It Takes At a Global Investment Conference in Lancaster House in London on July 26th 2012 Mario Draghi the president of the European Central Bank took the opportunity to make a brief but punchy speech. This was in quite a different style to the usual formal, dry and stylized statements made by central bankers at press conferences. The speech was laced with humour and contained some very frank comments.[5] The result was a turning point in peripheral spreads which from that point onwards fell back to much lower levels. Volatility in the US fell from that point onwards too. This was the turning point for the sovereign crisis in Europe, although few people recognized it as such at the time. What came across was the utter determination to keep the euro currency and union together, using "whatever it takes" within the remit of the central bank. But what hammered the message home was the rejoinder "and believe me, it will be enough". Also he pointed out that he believed it was within his remit to bring down the funding costs of peripheral countries. Both these key points are in bold below:

I asked myself what sort of message I want to give to you; I wouldn't use the word "sell", but actually I think the best thing I could do, is to give you a candid assessment of how we view the euro situation from Frankfurt.

And the first thing that came to mind was something that people said many years ago and then stopped saying it: The euro is like a bumblebee. This is a mystery of nature because it shouldn't fly but instead it does. So the euro was a bumblebee that flew very well for several years. And now – and I think people ask "how come?" – probably there was something in the atmosphere, in the air, that made the bumblebee fly. Now something must have changed in the air, and we know what after the financial crisis. The bumblebee would have to graduate to a real bee. And that's what it's doing.

The first message I would like to send, is that the euro is much, much stronger, the euro area is much, much stronger than people acknowledge today. Not only if you look over the last 10 years but also if you look at it now, you see that as far as inflation, employment, productivity, the euro area has done either like or better than US or Japan.

Then the comparison becomes even more dramatic when we come to deficit and debt. The euro area has much lower deficit, much lower debt than these two countries. And also not less important, it has a balanced current account, no deficits, but it also has a degree of social cohesion that you wouldn't find either in the other two countries.

---

[5]http://www.ecb.europa.eu/press/key/date/2012/html/sp120726.en.html

---

That is a very important ingredient for undertaking all the structural reforms that will actually graduate the bumblebee into a real bee.

The second point, the second message I would like to send today, is that progress has been extraordinary in the last six months. If you compare today the euro area member states with six months ago, you will see that the world is entirely different today, and for the better.

And this progress has taken different shapes. At national level, because of course, while I was saying, while I was glorifying the merits of the euro, you were thinking "but that's an average!", and "in fact countries diverge so much within the euro area, that averages are not representative any longer, when the variance is so big".

But I would say that over the last six months, this average, well the variances tend to decrease and countries tend to converge much more than they have done in many years - both at national level, in countries like Portugal, Ireland and countries that are not in the programme, like Spain and Italy.

The progress in undertaking deficit control, structural reforms has been remarkable. And they will have to continue to do so. But the pace has been set and all the signals that we get is that they don't relent, stop reforming themselves. It's a complex process because for many years, very little was done – I will come to this in a moment.

But a lot of progress has been done at supranational level. That's why I always say that the last summit was a real success. The last summit was a real success because for the first time in many years, all the leaders of the 27 countries of Europe, including UK etc., said that the only way out of this present crisis is to have more Europe, not less Europe.

A Europe that is founded on four building blocks: a fiscal union, a financial union, an economic union and a political union. These blocks, in two words – we can continue discussing this later – mean that much more of what is national sovereignty is going to be exercised at supranational level, that common fiscal rules will bind government actions on the fiscal side.

Then in the banking union or financial markets union, we will have one supervisor for the whole euro area. And to show that there is full determination to move ahead and these are not just empty words, the European Commission will present a proposal for the supervisor in early September. So in a month. And I think I can say that works are quite advanced in this direction.

So more Europe, but also the various firewalls have been given attention and now they are ready to work much better than in the past.

The second message is that there is more progress than it has been acknowledged.

But the third point I want to make is in a sense more political.

When people talk about the fragility of the euro and the increasing fragility of the euro, and perhaps the crisis of the euro, very often non-euro area member states or leaders, underestimate the amount of political capital that is being invested in the euro.

And so we view this, and I do not think we are unbiased observers, we think the euro is irreversible. And it's not an empty word now, because I preceded saying exactly what actions have been made, are being made to make it irreversible.

But there is another message I want to tell you.

Within our mandate, the ECB is ready to do whatever it takes to preserve the euro. And believe me, it will be enough.

There are some short-term challenges, to say the least. The short-term challenges in our view relate mostly to the financial fragmentation that has taken place in the euro area. Investors retreated within their national boundaries. The interbank market is not functioning. It is only functioning very little within each country by the way, but it is certainly not functioning across countries.

And I think the key strategy point here is that if we want to get out of this crisis, we have to repair this financial fragmentation.

There are at least two dimensions to this. The interbank market is not functioning, because for any bank in the world the current liquidity regulations make - to lend to other banks or borrow from other banks - a money losing proposition. So the first reason is that regulation has to be recalibrated completely.

The second point is in a sense a collective action problem: because national supervisors, looking at the crisis, have asked their banks, the banks under their supervision, to withdraw their activities within national boundaries. And they ring fenced liquidity positions so liquidity can't flow, even across the same holding group because the financial sector supervisors are saying "no".

So even though each one of them may be right, collectively they have been wrong. And this situation will have to be overcome of course.

And then there is a risk aversion factor. Risk aversion has to do with counterparty risk. Now to the extent that I think my counterparty is going to default, I am not going to lend to this counterparty. But it can be because it is short of funding. And I think we took care of that with the two big LTROs where we injected half a trillion of net liquidity into the euro area banks. We took care of that.

Then you have the counterparty recess related to the perception that my counterparty can fail because of lack of capital. We can do little about that.

Then there's another dimension to this that has to do with the premia that are being charged on sovereign states borrowings. These premia have to do, as I said, with default, with liquidity, but they also have to do more and more with convertibility, with the risk of convertibility. Now to the extent that these premia do not have to do with factors inherent to my counterparty - they come into our mandate. They come within our remit.

To the extent that the size of these sovereign premia hampers the functioning of the monetary policy transmission channel, they come within our mandate.

So we have to cope with this financial fragmentation addressing these issues.

I think I will stop here; I think my assessment was candid and frank enough.

Thank you.

September 2012 ECB OMT Hammering home the effects of the "whatever it takes" speech the European Central Bank announced on August 2nd that in emergencies it would buy the bonds of European sovereign nations directly in order to push down their yields. This generosity came with "conditionality": countries seeking such a bailout would have to yield to a macroeconomic adjustment programme overseen by the IMF. This ensured that they would endeavour to cut their spending to get their debt level under control. If the sovereign failed to comply with the adjustment programme by spending too much or dragging its feet over reform this aid would be withdrawn. The bond purchases were called Outright Monetary Transactions (OMT). The ECB's primary role is to ensure that there is price stability in the euro zone (targeting inflation at just below 2%) and buying bonds would have increased the supply of money fuelling inflation. Consequently each euro that entered the financial system as the ECB bought bonds through OMT was reabsorbed by issuing deposits, a process called sterilization. The OMT programme combined with "whatever it takes" was the crisis turning point that brought sovereign yields down to manageable levels and broke the link between US equity volatility and European government bond yields.

How to spot the turning point in a crisis

There are old-fashioned tried and tested crisis indicators and there are new indicators which are now available thanks to advances in technology. The old indicators suffer from being updated infrequently, and the new indicators from being unproven. Precisely which indicators matter will depend on the nature of the crisis. For example in an oil crisis the key indicator is the price of oil whereas a housing crisis would focus on house prices. However share prices and volatility are always affected by corporate earnings, so indicators that reflect changes in the business climate are the generic indicators that we will look at because they are always useful. And we will only deal here with indicators that are easily available to anyone with Internet access, because some crisis indicators are proprietary and require a hefty subscription.

Any single indicator will not work on its own. For example consumer sentiment stopped falling in June 2008 and rose steeply for three months, then fell sharply in October 2008 following the collapse of Lehman. By looking for turning points in many indices it is possible to build a better picture of when volatility will start to fall and stocks will start to rise again. One of the best timed trades I have heard of after the collapse of Lehman was by Frank Velling, Chief Strategist at BankInvest, who went heavily overweight equities at *precisely* the right time in March 2009. Many will recall the terror of systemic collapse of markets at the time, so Frank's call was both insightful and courageous. This is how he went about finding the turning point in his own words:

> Despite the extreme volatility in equity markets during the first months of 2009, it was obvious to me that the inflection point from a fundamental market view of the economy had occurred already on November 21st, 2008. I based that conclusion on three observations from that day: (i) **VIX** peaked that day, (ii) **Emerging Market Bond Index (EMBI) spread** peaked and (iii) the **break-even inflation** on 10 year Treasury Inflation Protected Securities (TIPS) bottomed. Not until later was it obvious that the

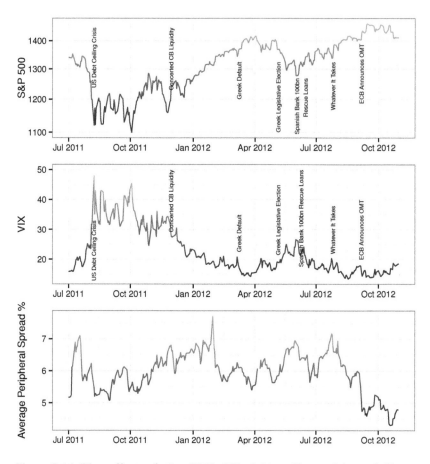

Figure 2.14: The effect of the 2011 US debt ceiling crisis and European sovereign debt crisis on the S&P 500 and VIX. Source: Bloomberg.

S&P 500 Homebuilders index actually bottomed the same day! Consequently I was looking for confirmation that the tsunami of monetary stimulus was having an effect, that we were near a capitulation point for the sell-off in equities and that the interbank market was showing signs of healing.

I looked specifically for clues from three sets of indicators: economic, market behaviour and banking. Pinpointing the inflection point for the market view of the economy gave me some comfort later on when I called the bottom for equity markets. The most important economic indicators are employment statistics, sentiment indicators and, during this specific period, housing indicators. Three indicators that were important in convincing me of a turnaround in equity markets in March 2009 were:

Economic indicators: my research showed that the turning point for equities during the previous five recessions occurred when the non-farm payrolls started to fall at a slower rate. However non-farm payrolls is notoriously volatile so this had to be supported by other employment indicators such as the weekly jobless claims. One of my favourite housing market indicators is a demand/supply indicator constructed using three statistics: existing home sales (demand) relative to the sum of building permits and the stock of unsold homes (supply). This indicator bottomed in December 2008.

Flow and sentiment: changes in the slope of the volatility curve and changes in the put-call ratio of S&P 500 options. When either the steepness of the VIX volatility term structure falls significantly from its long-term average or the put-call ratio of S&P 500 options is above its long-term average the chance of an equity recovery increases.

Banking: my preferred indicator was the spread between 3 month dollar LIBOR and OIS as an indicator of the interbank market.

Economic Crisis Indicators

A very valuable source of information for the US economy is the Federal Reserve Economic Data web site[6] (FRED) which also comes with a set of apps

---

[6]http://research.stlouisfed.org/fred

that allow you to search for, retrieve and download economic data. Where available I have included the FRED code for each variable.

Consumer Sentiment Indices The University of Michigan in collaboration with Thompson Reuters publishes a consumer sentiment index each month (FRED identifier UMCSENT). The index is based on 50 questions answered by US consumers in at least 500 telephone interviews. The questions are about each interviewee's own finances and their view on the short-term and long-term outlook for the economy. The value of the index was set at 100 in December 1966.

Purchasing Manager Indices PMIs are surveys sent each month to private companies where they are asked to answer a set of questions about their business. Each aspect of the business which is assessed has three possible values: deteriorating, the same, or improving. This is converted to a number between 0 (all respondents report deterioration) and 100 (all respondents report improvement). When the PMI is above 50 this indicates improvement, less than 50 is deterioration. The "headline" PMI is a composite of five components which are, in decreasing order of importance: new orders, output, employment, supplier delivery times and stocks of purchases. Regionally the important PMIs are the the US Institute of Supply Management (the ISM PMI, FRED identifier NAPM), PMIs produced by the market data company Markit,[7] the Bank of Japan's Tankan survey,[8] and the German Ifo index .[9]

Credit Availability Credit is like chocolate. A little bit is good for the economy, as it allows people and companies to borrow and spend. Too much can cause the economy to overheat and may inflate asset price bubbles. There then follows a painful period of "de-levering" when the debts are repaid (good) or default (bad) and this cools economic growth or causes outright crashes in asset prices. One of the many ways of measuring credit availability is to add up all the commercial and industrial loans from banks (FRED identifier EVANQ).

Wealth Effect Three factors are of key importance when making consumers, particularly US consumers, feel wealthy: the price of their house, the

---

[7]http://markiteconomics.com

[8]http://www.boj.or.jp/en/statistics/tk

[9]http://www.cesifo-group.de/ifoHome

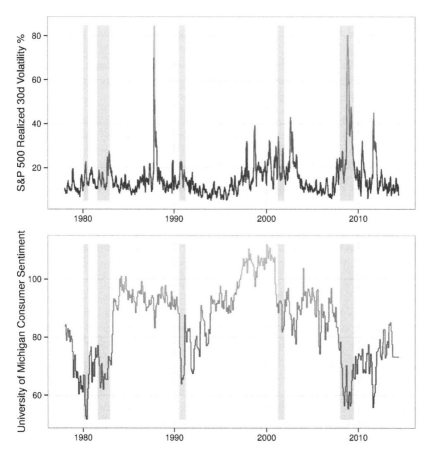

Figure 2.15: University of Michigan Consumer Sentiment and S&P 500 realized volatility. Shaded regions indicate recessions. Sharp falls in
consumer sentiment often coincide with periods of high volatility and as sentiment improves volatility usually subsides. Source:
Bloomberg.

price of their shares and the price of gasoline. Feeling wealthy is likely to make consumers spend more, and this is the engine of economic growth.

House Prices The monthly Case-Shiller index of house prices (FRED identifier SPCS20RSA) measures the average house price in 20 major US cities. To measure how homebuilding shares in the S&P 500 are performing there is an S&P 500 sub-index SPHOME which is tracked by an ETF with ticker XHB.[10]

Gasoline An average of gasoline prices based on a sample of approximately 900 retail outlets is published weekly by the US Department of Energy. This is the US Regular All Formulations Gas Price (FRED identifier GASREGW).

Share Price The S&P 500 share index is available on Yahoo finance with the ticker ^GSPC.

Inflation Inflation is the rate at which the cost of goods and services is changing (FRED identifier CPIAUCSL). The rate of inflation is measured by calculating the change in price of a standard basket of goods (calculated by the Bureau of Labour Statistics[11]). Inflation, like credit, is best when it is around 2%. Negative inflation (deflation) is a very worrying state of affairs as prices are continually falling which is a drag on corporate earnings. Too much inflation, above about 5% for the US, also causes share valuations to fall. Turning points in inflation expectations, as Frank Velling pointed out, can also be used as a useful indicator of the state of the economy. One way to measure inflation expectations is to take away the yield of inflation-linked bonds, whose coupons are linked directly to inflation, with US Treasuries of the same maturity. The difference between the two roughly reflects inflation expectations over the lifetime of the bonds and is called break-even inflation. For example to work out ten year break-even inflation take the ten year US Treasury bond yield (FRED identifier DGS10) and subtract the yield of US Treasury Inflation-Indexed Security (FRED identifier DFII10).

Leading Indicators As their name suggests these indices are combinations of economic variables which try to predict other economic variables, such as GDP. They are *not* leading indicators for market variables like

---

[10]http://finance.yahoo.com/q?s=XHB

[11]http://stats.bls.gov/cpi/cpifaq.htm

---

share prices and volatility. However they are useful, and their components are collectively informative about the health of the economy. The Federal Reserve Bank of Philadelphia produces monthly updates of a US leading indicator (available from FRED with identifier USSLIND). The Conference Board Leading Indicator is also widely used, and the OECD produces leading indicators for many countries. Leading indicators include variables such as:

Building permits for new private housing units Increasing demand for new houses leads to more building permit applications and this is a sign of economic health (available from FRED with identifier PERMIT).

Initial unemployment claims Increasing unemployment claims show that companies are cutting back their workforce because they expect falling demand so this is a negative indicator (available from FRED with identifier M08927USM548NNBR). Another closely watched indicator of employment is the non-farm payrolls number which measures the number of new jobs created each month (FRED identifier PAYEMS).

Vendor delivery performance Slower deliveries are a negative indicator. This is available from the National Association of Purchasing Management Survey (available from FRED with identifier M06006USM156NNBR).

Yield curve steepness Ten year yield minus Fed funds rate. Just as we found for the volatility term structure the "normal" shape of the yield curve for interest rates is upward-sloping. When the curve inverts (short-term rates are higher than long-term rates) this is usually a bearish indicator that is often followed by a recession. You can calculate the yield curve steepness by subtracting the Fed funds rate (available from FRED with identifier FEDFUNDS) from the ten year maturity Treasury bond yield (FRED identifier DGS10).

Average hours worked in manufacturing The larger the average hours worked the better, as companies will cut back hours if demand falls (FRED identifier AWHMAN).

Manufacturers' new orders for consumer goods and materials Increasing new orders for consumer goods shows greater demand for products and is a positive signal (FRED identifier ACDGNO).

Manufacturers' new orders for non-defense capital goods Capital goods are used to produce other goods, and include things such as machinery, factories and tools and equipment (FRED identifier NEWORDER). If companies are ordering more capital goods it is a positive signal because it suggests that companies expect more demand for their goods.

US dollar exchange rate with major trading partners When the dollar weakens relative to the currencies of its trading partners this is broadly positive for the economy because it cheapens the price of US exports making them more competitive and boosts foreign revenue when converted back into dollars (FRED identifier TWEXB). However a weak dollar also increases the price of imports such as oil.

Money supply Money supply is the total amount of money in the economy. The measures are numbered as the definition of "money" gets broader: M0 (notes and coins in circulation), M1 (M0 plus bank reserves), M2 (M1 plus various types of bank deposits and traveller's cheques) and so on. M2 is usually the money supply measure used in leading indicators, and its rise an fall are in theory linked with inflation (FRED identifier M2). The Fed itself doubts whether money supply is a useful measure, as Alan Greenspan (Fed Chairman from 1987 to 2002) said to the Committee on Banking and Financial Services in 2000:[12]

"The problem we have is not that money is unimportant, but how we define it. By definition, all prices are indeed the ratio of exchange of a good for money. And what we seek is what that is. Our problem is, we used M1 at one point as the proxy for money, and it turned out to be very difficult as an indicator of any financial state. We then went to M2 and had a similar problem. We have never done it with M3 per se, because it largely reflects the extent of the expansion of the banking industry, and when, in effect, banks expand, in and of itself it doesn't tell you terribly much about what the real money is.

So our problem is not that we do not believe in sound money; we do. We very much believe that if you have a debased currency that you will have a debased economy. The difficulty is in defining what part of our liquidity structure is truly money. We have had trouble ferreting out proxies for that for a number of years. And the standard we employ is whether it gives us a good forward indicator of the direction of finance and the economy. Regrettably none of those that we have been able to develop, including MZM, have done that. That does not mean that we think that money is irrelevant; it means that we think that our measures of money have been inadequate and as a consequence of that we, as I have mentioned previously, have downgraded the use of the monetary aggregates for monetary policy purposes until we are able to find a more stable proxy for what we believe is the underlying money in the economy."

---

[12]http://commdocs.house.gov/committees/bank/hba62930.000/hba62930_0f.htm

---

Share prices Rising share prices are a sign that earnings are increasing and the economy is performing well, although this can be misleading. For example during the lead-up to the dot-com bubble bursting share prices in the technology sector were built on a sense of euphoria rather than fundamental valuation. However a turn-around in stocks is an indicator that volatility will fall and has the benefit that share prices are updated daily.

Index of consumer expectations Consumer sentiment drives final demand for goods and services, and so is key to turning around the economy after a slump. The University of Michigan Consumer Sentiment Index, mentioned above, is one such index (FRED identifier UMCSENT).

Yields for corporate bonds Companies borrow money in the bond market. The interest rate at which they can borrow is measured as a yield and depends on the credit quality of the company. The riskier the borrower the greater their cost of borrowing (see Table 2.1 which details rating scales for Moody's, S&P and Fitch). When there is an economic crisis these funding costs increase as the probability of bankruptcy increases. To monitor credit risk the Baa yield is useful because it marks the lowest investment grade credit rating that is just one notch above junk (FRED identifier BAA). Some people look at the credit spread, or difference in yield, between government bonds and credit bonds as this measures the extra income demanded by bond investors to compensate them for the risk of default.

Crisis key words in social media

In each crisis the key words that drive volatility will change. Google monitors the frequency of search terms and provides access to this information in Google Trends.[13] In the period between 2007 and 2009 the level of VIX was matched closely by the frequency with with people searched for the term "Credit Crisis", as shown in Figure 2.17. Just as markets recovered from the credit crisis the European sovereign debt crisis began. The phrase "sovereign debt crisis" first shows up as a common search phrase in February 2010. After

---

[13]http://www.google.com/trends

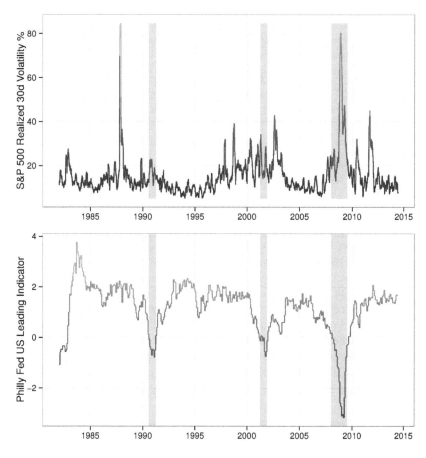

Figure 2.16: Federal Reserve Bank of Philadelphia's US Leading Indicator
and S&P 500 realized volatility. Sharp falls can precede a recession and high volatility, and when the leading indicator bounces
back growth should return and volatility should fall. Shaded regions indicate recessions. Source: Bloomberg.

this date the frequency of that search term in Google correlates very strongly with the level of VIX as the credit crisis fades in importance.

It is interesting that during the Flash Crash in 2010 there was a surge in the number of searches for the term "Sovereign Debt Crisis" even though that was not the cause of the sell-off. This may simply be because when people see share prices falling they want to know why. The first thing they do is google for "crisis". During the sovereign debt crisis the lumps and bumps in VIX match the popularity of "Sovereign Debt Crisis" very closely.

As a volatility investor you should have a list of the current crisis key words, and closely monitor the VIX index. We can use our sleeping dragon metaphor for volatility. Remember that when VIX is at 20% the dragon is asleep, 30% is one eye open and VIX at 40% means the dragon is completing its pre-flight checks and taxiing down the runway ready for takeoff. If VIX is at 30% and rising and all the crisis keywords are cropping up in the news headlines, then this is a strong reason to buy volatility. The time to sell volatility might be a decisive policy action by one or more central banks, or announcement of a massive government bailout, or some form of legal resolution that dampens the crisis. Every crisis is different and the only way to know the key words is to read the financial press.

Summary

News drives volatility The focus is on corporate earnings, particularly US corporate earnings in the case of VIX. A war in the the Central African Republic will have a marginal impact on US earnings whereas a war in the Middle East would affect the price of oil which would impact US earnings and volatility.

Drivers Some recurring themes can be counted on to increase volatility: popping of valuation bubbles, war, recession and central bank policy, big bankruptcies, politics, natural disasters, terrorism, flash crashes.

Timing: when to buy vol Volatility often takes a while to wake up to the existence of a crisis. In 2008 following the September 15th default of Lehman, VIX did not peak until November 20th. This gave investors plenty of time to buy volatility.

Timing: when to sell vol How do you spot crisis turning points? Following a large crisis recession often follows. There are many freely available

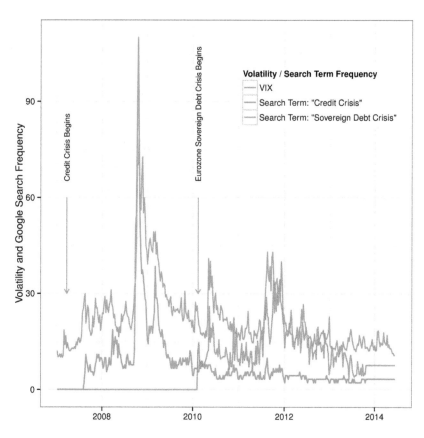

Figure 2.17: VIX alongside the popularity of searches on Google for "Credit Crisis" and "Sovereign Debt Crisis". Source: Bloomberg, Google.

economic indicators in the US and elsewhere which help spot improvement. VIX itself is useful, but so are GDP growth and inflation, leading indicators, purchasing manager indices rising above 50, and consumer and business sentiment indicators.

Crisis key words Both Google and Twitter allow users to monitor the popularity of search terms and hash tags. VIX is strongly tied to the number of searches for the crisis of the day. As the number of searches fade so does volatility.

3 How to invest in volatility

I don't know what's right and what's real any more
And I don't know how I'm meant to feel any more
When do you think it will all become clear?
'Cause I'm being taken over by the Fear

Lily Allen - The Fear

Professional investors will have many ways of buying or selling volatility.[1] For private investors, such as you and I, the choices are more limited. As always in investment it is best to invest only in things that you understand. I will focus here on the simplest way to buy and sell volatility, which is to buy an Exchange Traded Product (ETP) that is very closely linked to the volatility of stock prices. Behind the scenes the company that sells you the volatility ETP will be continually buying and selling the more complicated derivatives to make sure the ETP matches a volatility index. As usual the US market is the innovator with volatility ETPs so that many volatility ETPs are linked to VIX, which is a measure of US stock price volatility.

The most commonly traded type of exchange traded product is called an Exchange Traded Fund or ETF. A variant on an exchange traded *fund* is an exchange traded *note* (ETN). It is important to understand the difference between an ETF and ETN because almost all volatility exchange traded products are in the form of an ETN. ETNs carry an added risk over that of ETFs which is the *credit risk* of the issuer. What this means is that when you hand your money to an ETN issuer, the money and the assets that it buys belong to the issuer. With an ETF the money and assets still belong to you and are simply managed by the issuer so that bankruptcy of the issuer is just an inconvenience as some other manager can take over the fund and you lose none of your capital. If an ETN issuer, which is often an investment bank, goes bankrupt you may lose a significant proportion of your capital.

---

[1] To learn about buying and selling volatility with options (calls, puts, variance swaps and strategies such as straddles and strangles see my introductory book for finance professionals called "A Financial Bestiary".

Of course it is very unlikely that a large investment bank will go bankrupt, but after the Credit Crisis this is a risk that cannot be ignored. As the word "note" suggests, an ETN is a loan to the issuer, rather like a bond, with the promise that the principal value of the bond will track some index. If markets become concerned about the credit quality of the ETN issuer, the value of your ETN may fall irrespective of the value of its underlying assets. This reflects the market perception that the issuer will falter on its promise of repayment. The benefit of some ETNs is that the issuer can guarantee that the value of the ETN will match the value of its index perfectly because the issuer will make up a shortfall out of its own funds.

Benefits and Drawbacks of ETPs

Exchange traded products have benefits and risks, and it pays to know what these are before you invest. Here we briefly summarize the benefits and the drawbacks.

Benefit: Liquidity

An ETP looks just like a share, which means that you can buy and sell the ETP as often as you like through your share trading account. This easy buying and selling is important because if the value of your ETP starts to fall you want to be sure that you can find someone to buy it from you. Easy buying and selling is called liquidity, and another benefit of liquidity is a smaller difference between the price at which you buy and sell. If you are continually buying and selling shares you should be aware of the difference between the buying and selling prices because it can be a significant cost. Buying and selling prices for stocks in the S&P 500 usually differ by around 0.05%, whereas illiquid bonds can have differences of more than 1%.

Benefit: Market Access

As well as providing liquidity, ETPs can provide access to markets that might be unavailable to small investors. The minimum investment size for assets can be very large, but an ETP makes it possible to trade in much smaller amounts that are within the reach of most investors. Until the advent of exchange traded products investors had to pool their funds into mutual funds in order to get access to such markets. Now it is possible to trade commodities as Exchange Traded Commodities (ETCs exist for gold, silver, palladium, platinum, oil, grains, livestock, cocoa, coffee, sugar, hogs, livestock), bonds (government bonds, corporate bonds, inflation-linked bonds) and commercial property. And of course this book owes its existence to ETPs that allow small investors access to VIX futures which were previously only available to institutional investors.

In addition to providing access to new asset classes, ETPs have opened the doors to equity and bond markets geographically. Small investors in the US who were restricted to buying only US stocks from their broker can now buy ETPs which track stock indices for almost any country. An investor in Louisiana can buy an ETP that tracks stock prices in Indonesia or Peru just as easily as buying shares in Walmart.

Drawback: Fees

The first drawback of exchange traded products is that the company that manages them has to make a profit. This means you will be charged some fee that is subtracted from the return on the product. For example if you buy a gold bar you will have exposure to the gold price. If you buy an ETF that is linked to the price of gold you will also have exposure to the gold price, but the return on your investment will have a small amount subtracted, such that a 5% increase in the price of gold over a year would only pay, say, 4.5% for the gold ETF. The fees on exchange traded products vary widely, so it pays to read the small print on marketing material to find the word "fee". Generally the fee is around 0.4% each year for ETFs that track the price of equity and bond indices and commodity prices like oil and wheat. Fees are highest where the issuer is doing more fancy work such as a quantitative investment strategy or paying a human fund manager to invest on your behalf. Here the charge may be upwards of 2% each year for some products. A snapshot of fees for all VIX exchange traded products in 2013 shows that they are comparable with conventional exchange traded funds:

Minimum Annual Fee	0.36%
Average Annual Fee	0.85%
Maximum Annual Fee	1.15%

In 2012 half of the VIX ETPs had annual fees in the range 0.85% to 0.95%. This means that if you invest $100 in a volatility ETP you will lose a little less than a dollar each year to your fund manager regardless of activity in the volatility market. This sets a minimum barrier that you have to beat to break even, and is an important consideration when buying an ETF. The general rule for fees is that the managers must earn their fees. If the fund is doing something clever, which some volatility ETFs do as we shall see, then the manager can demand a higher fee. But if they are tracking VIX-related indices the fee should be at the lower end of the range.

Drawback: Tracking Error

The second drawback of exchange traded products is that they do not track their index perfectly. This is called tracking error. In other words, if you own an ETF that is supposed to track the S&P 500 share index you will often find that price movements of the ETF will not match those of the index. The S&P 500 may go up 10% and your ETF may go up 8%. This might be the effect of fees, or it might be some bad hedging on the part of the ETF provider.

To see how bad hedging can increase ETF tracking error a thought experiment may help. Imagine for a moment that you are an ETF provider and you are given $1 billion to manage in your S&P 500 ETF fund. Your clients want the value of their initial $1 billion to match the rise and fall of the S&P 500 stock index. The simplest way of making sure your fund matches the S&P 500 perfectly is to buy a portfolio of the 500 US stocks that match the contents and weights of the S&P 500. However some stocks, usually the smaller companies, do not trade so frequently as others. Lower liquidity means higher transaction costs. Remember that when you buy a stock you see two prices: the price at which you buy (offer price, which is higher) and sell (bid price, which is lower). The difference between the buy and sell price, the bid-offer spread, will be greatest for the least liquid, less frequently traded stocks. So you could miss out some of the illiquid stocks in the index and jiggle the remaining weights so that you still match the overall price of the S&P 500. This would reduce your transaction costs and increase your profit as an ETF manager. However this might increase your tracking error if you jiggle your stock weights incorrectly. ETF tracking errors vary, but a very large tracking error should ring alarm bells. Tracking error is something to watch out for when investigating ETF investments, often illustrated with a historical chart of the index versus the value of the ETF.

There is a way to have zero tracking error but this also comes with its own risks. Using our previous example, it is possible for our fund manager to take the $1 billion fund and use derivatives to track the price of the S&P 500. The fund manager can invest in S&P 500 futures. An S&P 500 future is an agreement to buy the S&P 500 index at a fixed price at a fixed date in the future. The important thing is that the price of the future tracks the S&P 500 almost perfectly. From the fund manager's point of view the future has a huge benefit over buying a basket of stocks, which is leverage. To track a $1 billion's worth of S&P 500 the fund manager only has to hand over a fraction of the total investment, sometimes as little as 10%. This means that the fund manager is left holding a $900 million cash fund that they can invest in other securities which may not be the S&P 500. The fund manager could invest the excess cash in very safe bonds, like US Treasuries, with low risk and low return. Alternatively the manager could invest in highly speculative trades with high risk and potentially higher returns. The ETF fund manager will pass on the return on the S&P 500 to their ETF investors. However any extra profit they make on the spare cash belongs to their fund management company. Some investors don't like the fund management using their capital in this way and only buy ETFs where any investments are strictly limited to low-risk securities.

As an ETF investor you will want to know whether the ETF is buying the physical thing it is tracking, so you may have to do some digging in the product prospectus. The ETF provider will often use words like "physical" to show that it is not using derivatives to track its index. If it is using derivatives the ETF description will sometimes have the label "synthetic". If synthetic it should describe the type of securities in which it is allowed to invest with its excess capital. Sometimes futures will not track the index very accurately, and we will see an example later where one volatility ETF was so popular it came to dominate and distort the volatility market and its tracking error ballooned as a result. For volatility ETFs the physical/synthetic distinction is irrelevant as it is impossible to track the value of VIX without using derivatives in some form.

Under the Hood of Volatility ETPs

You may be wondering why volatility products are so complicated. Why not just create a product that tracks VIX? The reason is that it is near to impossible to buy VIX directly. VIX can be replicated by buying a giant portfolio of options on individual shares in the S&P 500 stock index but this would be a very expensive product to manage for the issuer as they continually bought and sold options. It is much cheaper for them to buy futures on the VIX index as these track VIX very closely and therefore do most of the work for the product manager. The behaviour of your VIX ETP may be confusing if you think it tracks VIX. For example even though VIX rises slightly the value of your VIX exchange traded product may still fall. If you understand VIX futures you will understand VIX products, so in this section we go into the behaviour of VIX futures in just enough detail to understand the behaviour of VIX exchange traded products.

Short-Term and Mid-Term volatility futures

If you buy a future on the VIX the question then becomes: which future? Remember that a future is an agreement to buy something at a fixed price and at a fixed *date* in the future. VIX futures trade in maturities measured in months, up to nine months ahead. The most commonly traded futures are the shorter maturities. However VIX futures do not track VIX perfectly—they have an in-built tracking error. Generally the longer the expiry date of the VIX future the greater its tracking error. To understand short-term and mid-term volatility exchange traded products it pays to have a rough understanding of what drives their returns. The drivers are two-fold: the first one is exactly what you expect, the second is understood by very few investors.

VIX movements If the value of VIX increases sharply then all the VIX futures prices will rise, and if VIX falls sharply all the VIX futures prices will fall. The shorter the expiry of the futures contract, the bigger the rise and fall.

Roll Cost To maintain exposure to VIX each day the issuer has to sell a fraction of their shorter-dated futures contract and buy a longer-dated futures contract. If the longer-dated contract costs more than the sale price of the shorter-dated contract it will cost money to roll. Roll cost therefore depends on the *steepness* of the volatility term structure curve. The longer the expiry of the futures contracts the smaller the roll cost between two futures contracts as the curve is flatter further out on the curve. This roll cost will lose money during "normal" market conditions. Only in extreme crises does the roll cost turn positive as volatility term structure inverts.

These two drivers of return differentiate the behaviour of short and mid-term futures volatility products. Short-term volatility products will have greater sensitivity to VIX but come with a higher roll cost than mid-term volatility products. If you are completely convinced that VIX is about to sky-rocket in the near future then you would buy a short-term VIX futures exchange traded product because it will generate a greater profit when VIX rises. If you think that VIX may take a while to spike then mid-term products might be better because their roll cost is lower. The price you pay is that if VIX does spike the mid-term products will generate a smaller return than their short-term counterparts. To summarize:

	Short-term VIX futures	Mid-term VIX futures
Roll cost	Higher (bad)	Lower (good)
VIX Sensitivity	Higher (good)	Lower (bad)

The roll cost and sensitivity differences are shown clearly by looking at two VIX volatility exchange traded products in Figure 3.1. These are VXX, which is a short-term VIX exchange traded note, and VXZ, which is a mid-term VIX exchange traded note. To show the difference in roll cost the prices have been re-scaled such that they both start off at a value of 100 on February 20th 2009 and the daily prices are tracked over the next three and a half years. This is as if you had invested $100 in each index in 2009 and then tracked the values of these investments over time.

Firstly we ignore the bumps and spikes and focus on the long-term trends of each investment. Both volatility series re-iterate the fact that most volatility exchange traded products are not long-term investments because they are almost guaranteed to lose money over long periods of time. The short-term ETN (VXX) is falling in price much more quickly than the mid-term ETN (VXZ). This is because the roll cost of the short-term product is much higher than the mid-term product. VXX would have lost 97% of your investment over this period (an annual loss of 65%) and VXZ would have lost 61% (an annual loss of 24%). The rent for holding short-term VIX futures is much higher than the rent for mid-term VIX futures.

Looking at the bumps and spikes now, the short-term VIX ETN (VXX) is much more responsive to spikes in volatility than the mid-term VIX ETN (VXZ). Figure 3.1 makes this sensitivity difficult to see because it is washed out by the strong long-term effect of roll cost. Observing a shorter period of time enhances the effect of the level of VIX and diminishes the effect of roll cost, so we can zoom in on the period between July 2011 and March 2012.

At the beginning of July 2011 VIX was hovering at around 16%, the S&P 500 share index was at 1340 and most market participants were on vacation. However there were reasons for concern. The European sovereign crisis, a consistent source of worrying news flow, was likely to provide another scare. At the same time the US Congress had to approve a measure to raise the debt ceiling. This turned into a protracted and very public squabble between Democrats and Republicans which spooked the markets. As people returned to their desks they decided that in the light of these systemic threats equity

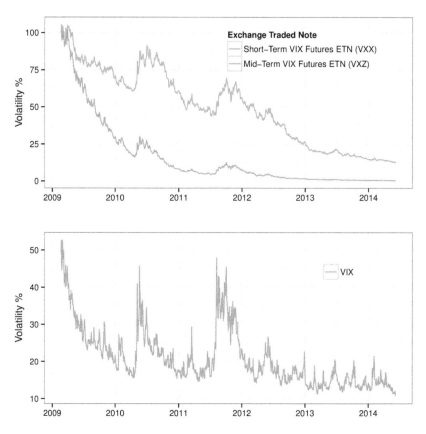

Figure 3.1: Re-scaled price of a short-term ETN (VXX) and mid-term ETN (VXZ) from February 2009 to August 2012. The short-term ETN loses value through roll cost much faster than the mid-term ETN. Source: Bloomberg.

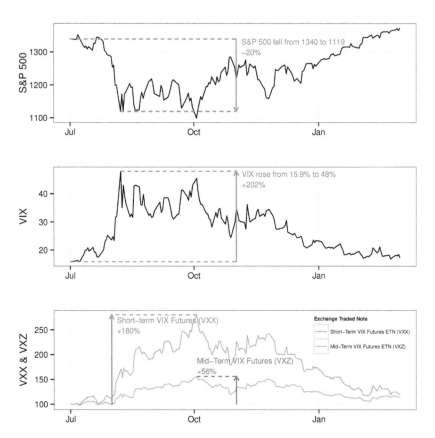

Figure 3.2: August 2011 share sell-off: S&P 500 stock index, VIX volatility index, short-term VIX (VXX) and mid-term VIX (VXZ) ETN prices from July 2011 to March 2012. The short-term ETN has greater sensitivity to VIX, and generates greater profit when VIX rises, than the mid-term ETN.

was too risky and sold their shares, with the S&P 500 falling from 1340 to 1120 by August 28th, a fall of 16% in just one month. As it turned out the debt ceiling was raised in time to avoid disaster but markets took six months to recover their lost ground. The effect of this sell-off on the S&P 500, VIX, and the short-term and mid-term VIX ETNs are shown in Figure 3.2.

During the protracted period of volatility during and after the August 2011 equity sell-off, the value of VIX rose rapidly from 16% to a peak of 48% on August 8th and stayed above 30% until the beginning of October. Looking at VXX and VXZ in Figure 3.2, they clearly gained in value during the initial volatility spike up to August 8th. The short-term VIX exchange traded note (VXX) gained much more in this period, rising 180% compared to a rise of just 56% for the mid-term note (VXZ). This greater VIX sensitivity is why people still buy VXX despite its rather brutal roll cost.

However the story does not end there. Remember that the returns on VXX and VXZ depend on two things: the level of VIX and roll cost. Roll cost turns *positive* during a crisis. In other words you get paid to hold VXX and VXZ during a crisis while the term structure of volatility remains inverted. Even if you missed the volatility boat on the equity sell-off that made VIX peak on August 8th, you could still have made another 63% return by buying volatility after this peak. This is because VXX did not peak until October 3rd. Similarly for VXZ you could have made another 29%. Volatility term structure inverts during only the worst crises but when it happens this gift of positive roll is something that the savvy volatility investor cannot ignore.

What is roll cost?

Given the importance of volatility term structure to the roll cost of many volatility exchange traded products, it is worth digging a bit deeper into this key concept. The reason why the product manager has to "roll" is that futures contracts expire. If the fund manager buys a one-month VIX future then after a month passes the future will expire. This must never happen because if the contract expires the fund will no longer have any sensitivity to VIX.

A useful mental picture is to imagine that VIX futures are like boxes on a conveyor belt. There are always nine VIX futures boxes on the VIX conveyor belt labeled "one" to "nine". When the "one" box falls off the end of the belt the labels are all reduced by one: box nine becomes box eight and a new box nine is placed on the belt. A short-term VIX futures exchange traded product manager must keep money in the last two boxes (box one and two) that are about to fall off the belt. As the one-month box on the belt creeps toward the precipice he will move a little of his money each day from box one (the one-month VIX future) into box two (the two-month VIX future). If he does this correctly then by the end of the expiry month there will be none of his money in the box that falls off the belt. Money has to be continually rolled in this way to keep exposure to volatility at all times.

Rolling means that the fund manager will be selling shorter-dated VIX futures and buying longer-dated VIX futures. Longer-dated VIX futures are usually more expensive than shorter-dated VIX futures, which means that the manager is selling a cheap contract and buying an expensive contract, and is losing money by rolling. In Figure 3.3 we can see three snapshots of the prices of VIX and the first seven futures contracts on three separate dates. VIX is a measure of stock volatility over the next 30 days. The one-month VIX future depends on the market view of stock volatility over the thirty-day period starting one month in the future. The two month VIX future depends on the market view of stock volatility over the thirty day period starting two months in the future, and so on along the curve. Each point on the curve depends on the market view of another term in the future, which is why this is called volatility "term structure".

The "normal" situation is the term structure on November 2006 where VIX is below 20 and the curve slopes gently upward. When VIX is very high the term structure inverts and becomes downward-sloping, and if VIX is close to its "resting" value of 20% the term structure is upward-sloping. Sometimes the market may expect turmoil in the future even though markets are calm, and in this case VIX can be low but the curve is sharply upward-sloping because investors expect VIX to increase in the coming months. This was the case in August 2012 and caused short-term and mid-term VIX exchange traded products to lose value very rapidly. However when VIX shoots up, as it did after the collapse of Lehman, investors rush to buy short-term protection and this pushes up the price of shorter-dated contracts. This leads to an inverted term structure, as we can see in November 2008. Rolling down this inverted curve the fund manager is selling the expensive one-month future and buying the cheaper two-month future, and the roll generates a profit.

Given the importance of VIX term structure it is frustrating that VIX futures prices are not available on free financial web sites such as Yahoo Finance and Google Finance. This information is not absolutely necessary however, as there is a strong relationship between the value of VIX and the term structure of volatility, as shown in Figure 3.4. Each point on the graph shows the one-month/two-month steepness versus the value of VIX for each trading day between 2004 and 2012. When VIX is below 31%, which it is 90% of the

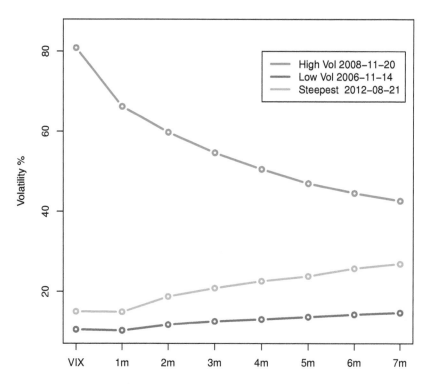

Figure 3.3: Volatility term structure under normal and crisis conditions. Source: Bloomberg.

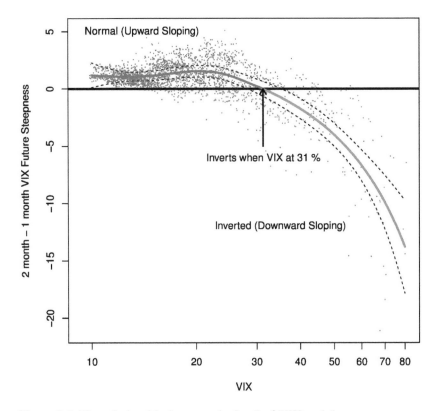

Figure 3.4: The relationship between the level of VIX and the term structure of VIX one month and two month futures. Source: Bloomberg.

time, then term structure is usually upward-sloping and rolling costs money. But if VIX exceeds 31%, which it is just 10% of the time, the term structure inverts, and the higher VIX rises the stronger the inversion of the curve and the greater the profit from rolling. This is why volatility investors could reap a roll profit in August and September 2011, because VIX remained elevated at 30% and above for a sustained period as fear of the US debt ceiling and the European sovereign crisis washed through markets.

How much does VIX have to rise to make a profit?

Choosing a volatility index is a trade-off between carry cost and sensitivity to VIX. Short-term VIX futures have a greater carry cost, which is bad, but greater sensitivity to VIX, which is good if VIX rises. This becomes very clear when we consider this in terms of monthly costs (Figure 3.5). The graph shows monthly change in VIX on the x axis and the return of the short-term, mid-term and dynamic VIX indices on the y axis.

Starting with sensitivity to VIX, the winner by far is the short-term VIX index which has a 320% sensitivity. This means that if VIX increases by 10% the short-term index increases in value by 32%. In contrast the mid-term index would gain just 14% and the dynamic VIX index just 11%. The average monthly cost for each index reflects the price of sensitivity: -2.5% for the short-term index, -0.3% for the mid-term and an average income of 1.8% for dynamic VIX. The upshot is that for long-term investors, dynamic VIX is the best choice. For short-term profit when you are certain that VIX will rise in the next few weeks, the short-term index is more appropriate.

Another way of thinking about the carry cost/sensitivity trade-off is in terms of stall speed. Aeroplanes must travel above a certain speed at all times otherwise their wings do not generate enough lift to keep them airborne. Similarly when you buy volatility, VIX must increase in order to generate a profit. At a certain VIX "speed" the profit will just balance the roll cost of your index. The question we can ask is: how much does VIX have to increase to pay off the carry cost and break even? In Figure 3.5 the stall speed is the VIX monthly percent change where each line crosses the y axis. For dynamic VIX, even a month in which VIX falls by -1.4% will break even. For the mid-term index, VIX has to increase by at least 0.3% to break even, and for the short-term index the stall speed is 0.8%. If VIX remains steady, then on average the short-term index will lose 2.7%, mid-term VIX will generate a tiny loss of 0.4% and the dynamic VIX index stands to generate a profit of 1.5%.

The final question is how many months we see positive returns for the three indices (see Table 3.1). Again, short-term VIX is the most extreme, making a monthly loss two-thirds of the time since 2006. Mid-term VIX loses money about 60% of the time and dynamic VIX has an even chance of making a profit or loss. Dynamic VIX is really the only choice if you want a VIX investment that breaks even on average over the long term but remember if you have an ETF or ETN you will have to pay fees of about 1% per year so even dynamic VIX exchange traded products will on average make a loss over the long term.

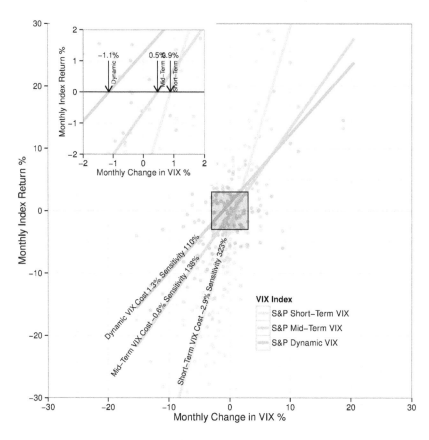

Figure 3.5: Monthly percent increase in VIX required to make a profit for short-term, mid-term and dynamic VIX indices. Source: Bloomberg.

	Short-Term	Mid-Term	Dynamic
Monthly Roll Cost	-2.7%	-0.4%	1.5%
VIX Sensitivity	322.%	139.%	111.%
VIX Monthly Stall Speed	0.8%	0.3%	-1.4%
Percent Positive Returns	34.0%	41.5%	48.9%

Table 3.1: Monthly stall speed, roll cost and VIX sensitivity for VIX indices. Data for the period from 2006-2013. Source: Bloomberg.

Reducing roll cost

In order to address the problem of the huge VIX futures roll cost, some VIX exchange traded products carry the word "dynamic" or "enhanced" in their title. A popular example goes under the ticker XVZ, which is the iPath S&P 500 Dynamic VIX exchange traded note. This ETN tracks the S&P 500 Dynamic VIX Futures index[2] which contains all the machinery to reduce roll cost and volatility to make a product that investors can buy and hold for longer periods of time.

The trick the dynamic VIX index employs is to switch its position in short-term and mid-term futures contracts depending on the shape of the volatility term structure. Under "normal" conditions the curve is upward-sloping and steepest for the one and two month part of the curve. Under these conditions the strategy shorts the one- and two-month part of the curve to earn carry. But it still needs to have overall positive exposure to VIX (it is a VIX index!) so it goes long the four- to seven-month part of the curve. When the curve is inverted rolling contracts becomes a benefit that is felt most strongly at the one- to two-month part of the curve, so the strategy flips its negative exposure in these contracts to positive exposure to earn the carry.

Just as a car has five gears for different speeds, the dynamic VIX index has five allocations that are each tuned to give optimal return for five different levels of VIX term structure (see Table 3.2). The strategy monitors VIX term structure each day, although it reallocates only when necessary to reduce trading costs. It measures term structure by comparing the ratio of VIX with the three-month VIX futures contract, ticker VXV. The VIX to VXV ratio is a useful one for non-professional investors because the value of VXV is available free of charge on web sites such as Yahoo Finance.

The value of VIX divided by three-month future VIX and the associated dynamic VIX index "gear" are illustrated in Figure 3.6. Almost all of the time is spent in the first and second gears where the term structure measure is below 1 (which means the curve is not inverted). The occasions when the curve inverts are rare such that gears 3, 4 and 5 are associated with periods of extreme crisis. Between 2008 and 2013 the curve was steeply upward-sloping most (58.2%) days. The remaining states occurred far less frequently: upward-sloping 33.4%, flat 5.1%, inverted 2.6% and steeply inverted 0.6%.

The documentation for the dynamic VIX index states that:

---

[2]Details on the precise method used to dynamically adjust the S&P dynamic VIX futures index are available from the S&P Dow Jones Indices site http://www.spindices.com/indices/strategy/sp-500-dynamic-vix-futures-tr.

Term Structure	Allocation	
VIX / 3m VIX	*Short-Term*	*Long -Term*
TS < 90%	-0.30	0.70
90% < TS < 100%	-0.20	0.80
100% < TS < 105%	0.00	1.00
105% < TS <115%	0.25	0.75
TS > 115%	0.50	0.50

Table 3.2: Dynamic VIX allocation based on term structure (VIX/VXV).

"The S&P Commodities Index Committee maintains the S&P 500 Dynamic VIX futures Indices. The committee meets regularly. At each meeting, the Index Committee reviews any significant market events. In addition the Index Committee may revise index policy for timing and rebalancings or other matters."

In other words the strategy may change if the governing committee at S&P decide that it is no longer well suited to market conditions. For example the definition of the gear ranges, the number of gears, or the allocations for each gear could change. But the spirit of the product, which is to create exposure to VIX while minimizing carry costs, will presumably remain intact.

The effect of dynamic reallocation by the dynamic VIX index is to reduce the roll cost of the product, and it achieves this well, as we can see in Figure 3.7. Notice that this graph only runs from August 2011 when XVZ was first issued. XVZ behaves more like a bond than a share, hovering around a value of 100 without much volatility. This is perfectly suited, and in fact designed, to be suitable for investors with a smaller risk appetite than those who would buy VXX and VXZ. If you think VIX is about to increase then you could buy XVZ and wait for a long time before being proven correct. If you are wrong, and even the most obstinate investor has to admit this is possible, then you do not lose money at an alarming rate. If you are right, however, the rise in value for XVZ is much smaller than an investment in short-term or mid-term VIX futures indices such as VXX and VXZ.

The S&P dynamic VIX index is not the only VIX futures index constructed to minimize roll costs. At the CBOE VIX microsite[3] you will find a few others in the "CBOE Customized Indexes" section. DLVIX and DSVIX are created

---

[3]http://www.cboe.com/micro

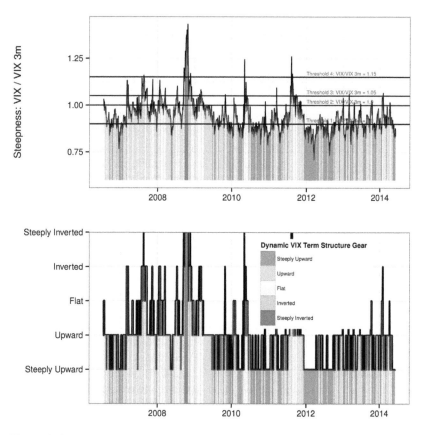

Figure 3.6: Steepness indicator (VIX/VXV) with four thresholds and associated dyamic VIX gear since 2010. Source: Bloomberg.

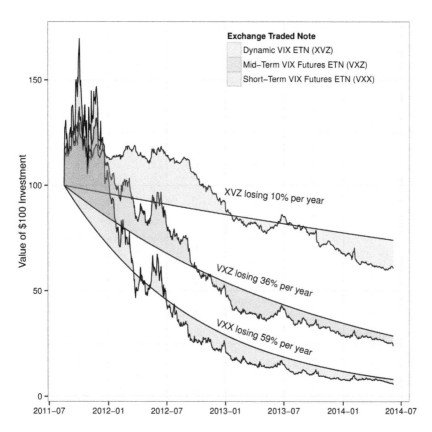

Figure 3.7: Comparison of long-term returns for XVZ (Dynamic VIX ETN) versus VXX (VIX Short-Term Futures ETN) and VXZ (VIX Mid-Term Futures ETN). Source: Bloomberg.

by Société Générale[4] to gain long and short exposure to VIX while maximizing roll benefits. Both use a VIX term structure and a VIX momentum component to determine their allocation to short-term and mid-term VIX futures. Société Générale has contracted with Chicago Board Options Exchange Incorporated to calculate and disseminate values of these indices.

JP Morgan has created their Macro Hedge Index which is again designed to provide long volatility exposure while aiming to reduce some of the costs associated with carrying such a position. The solution is similar to the others we have seen. The index uses long and an sometimes short positions in VIX futures, but also includes positions in European VSTOXX futures. The strategy is designed to generate positive returns under a wide variety of market conditions.

Long volatility and short volatility

If you think volatility is about to go up you buy it today at a low price and (hopefully) sell it later at a high price. In the language of investment, once you buy an ETP that gives exposure to volatility you are *long* volatility. But what would you do if you think volatility is about to fall? In this case you can go *short* volatility. If you are short volatility, you want volatility to go down because you sold it at a high price. Then you (hopefully) close out your position by buying volatility back at a lower price.

Some people get confused by shorting because it seems strange to sell something that you do not own. But that is the wrong way to think about short positions. Investing for profit means that you buy at a low price and sell at a high price. However you can do this in any order. Normally you buy something at a low price then sell at a high price but shorting means you can sell something at a high price then buy it back at a low price. Once you go long volatility or go short volatility this is your volatility *position*. We can summarize a long position and a short position as follows:

> **long vol position**: profit if volatility rises   usually lose from roll
> **short vol position**: profit if volatility falls   usually profit from roll

If you want a short position in volatility there are exchange traded products that use VIX futures to maintain a continual short position. For the ETP product manager this is as simple as reversing the trades for a long position.

---

[4]http://www.cboe.com/micro/dlvix

Instead of buying VIX futures they sell VIX futures. All the things we now understand about VIX futures now apply in reverse. To roll the *short* VIX position the issuer will be continually buying short-dated VIX futures contracts and selling long-dated VIX futures contracts. The roll cost will be reversed. Instead of having a position that loses money with near certainty over long time horizons, you will have a position that almost certainly makes money over long time horizons. The risk with a short volatility position is that there will be a volatility spike and the value of your short position will plummet as volatility rises. While volatility stays above about 30%, term structure will reverse and you will also lose money from rolling your position.

This is best explained by tracking the value of a $100 investment in a pair of volatility exchange traded products where one is long volatility and the other is short volatility. In Figure 3.8 we can see the value of our $100 invested either in VXX which is long volatility and SVXY which is short volatility. Over the period from October 2011 to October 2013 the long-term trends are very clear. VXX is losing money through roll cost and SVXY is gaining money through roll cost. The $100 invested in SVXY rose in value to $518 while VXX fell to $6. Over this period of time, smoothing out the bumps, SVXY was growing in value at a rate of 134% each year while VXX was losing 82% of its value each year.

On the face of it the obvious thing to do is buy SVXY because it seems like a sure bet. However it is not a smooth ride. Looking at the spiky events when volatility rose sharply, such as June 2012, we can see that SVXY lost value whereas VXX gained in value. Between the end of March and the beginning of June 2012 the tables were turned. The supposedly "sure bet" short volatility SVXY lost 39% while the long volatility VXX, which seems like a lame duck over the long term, gained 44%. We can see that volatility exchange traded products are themselves extremely volatile. If you want a long-term investment, and you are willing not to sleep well at night as you lose significant capital during periods of high volatility, then reaping the roll on VIX futures is something to consider through short-volatility exchange traded products like SVXY.

Note that being short volatility is not the same as being long stocks. This is because stocks are directional, which is to say that you only make money if stock prices rise. A short volatility position is indifferent about the sign of moves, it only cares about the size of moves. Short volatility profits from small daily moves and loses money when daily moves are large. Notice that short volatility does not care about drift either. S&P 500 share prices can drift upwards and SVXY can still profit as long as the daily moves remain small. This is usually the case in a strong and sustained bull market for stocks, hence the long-term attractiveness of SVXY when stock markets are performing well. A simple rule might be that if stocks are not mentioned in newspaper headlines or the main bulletins of TV news then SVXY will perform well.

Just in case you felt you were starting to understand how these VIX exchange traded products work, there is another thing to consider. You can choose different parts of the VIX term structure to be short, just as you can choose which part of the term structure to be long. The official name for the SVXY exchange traded fund is the "ProShares Short VIX Short-Term Futures ETF". Here, "short" means you have a short position in VIX futures, and "short-term" means that you are short the short-term futures contracts. Short-term usually means the one-month and two-month VIX futures contracts. This picture breaks down the official name of this ETF:

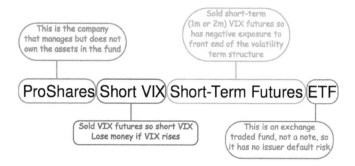

Leveraged volatility

If being long and short does not offer enough choice on your volatility menu, there is another even more exotic dimension in volatility exchange traded products: *leverage*. Instead of receiving or paying returns based on the movement of VIX futures you can receive multiples of these returns. If you have a two times levered long VIX exchange traded product you will earn and lose twice as much as someone with a regular VIX exchange traded product without any leverage. Leverage can sometimes increase your return if you are right about the direction of volatility. However leverage *always* increases your risk and can make your losses very severe if you are wrong about the direction of volatility. These are products for investors with a huge appetite for risk.

Figure 3.9 compares the value of $100 invested in the VXX exchange traded product, which is long and has no leverage, and UVXY which has two times

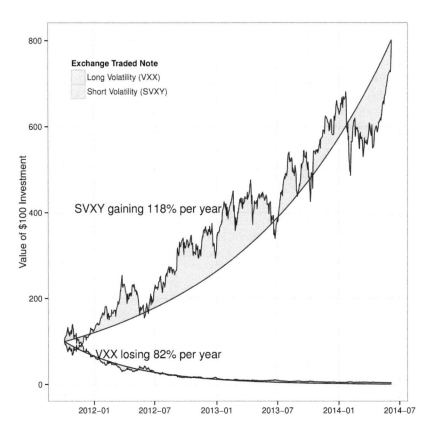

Figure 3.8: Value of a $100 investment in SVXY (short volatility) and VXX (long volatility) from October 2011 to September 2012. Source: Bloomberg.

leverage. As we saw previously, over the long term VXX loses about 82% per year through roll cost. UVXY was losing 99.1% of its value per year over this period. All the arguments about long volatility being a short-term investment just before a crisis apply twice as strongly to the levered product. If you could bear to hold your position in VXX for one month then you could only afford to hold UVXY for two weeks. On the other hand if you buy UVXY just before volatility spikes you would make roughly twice the profit that you would with VXX.

Think of leverage as a daily return multiplier. If VIX goes up 10% in one day, an ETP without leverage also rises by roughly 10%. A short ETP would fall 10%, and a two times levered ETP would gain 20%. These three choices are illustrated in Figure 3.10. Each point in the figure is the percentage daily change of VIX on the x axis versus the daily percentage change in either VXX (leverage +100%), SVXY (leverage -100%) or UVXY (leverage +200%) on the y axis. The graph highlights the days when VIX rises 10% using a dashed vertical bar. VXX rises one for one with VIX because its leverage is 100% and you can see that when VIX rises 10% VXX also rises by 10%. SVXY is short VIX, such that a return of +10% for VIX results in a return of -10% for SVXY. UVXY is two times levered, so that a VIX return of +10% will give a +20% return in UVXY. The slope of each line is the leverage: the slope is +1 for VXX, -1 for SVXY and +2 for UVXY.

Figure 3.10 shows that over the time scale of one day the long-term downward drift due to carry cost becomes all but invisible and the return is driven almost entirely by daily movements in VIX. To see why this is so, consider the size of drift. If VXX is losing about 90% of its value each year, then as there are about 260 trading days in a year this is a daily loss of 90%/260 or about 0.3%. Compare this tiny drift with the average daily change in VIX, which is about 6%, and it is clear that the daily change of VIX will drown out drift over a single day because it is twenty times larger. If you are sharp eyed you will notice that the points in Figure 3.10 have a tendency to lie below the straight lines. This is most pronounced for UVXY and SVXY. The result of this sag is that you gain a little less profit when your ETP rises and lose a little more when your ETP falls compared against a yardstick of a perfect long or short VIX ETP. This leads nicely to the next section on tracking error.

What can go wrong with ETPs?

Exchange traded products have revolutionized the world of investment by bringing whole groups of asset classes into the reach of individual investors.

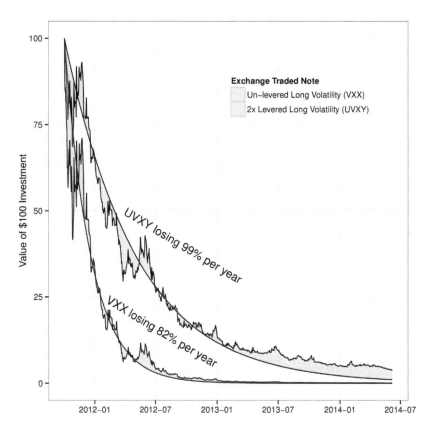

Figure 3.9: Value of a $100 investment in UVXY (2x levered volatility) and VXX (long volatility) from October 2011 to February 2014. Source: Bloomberg.

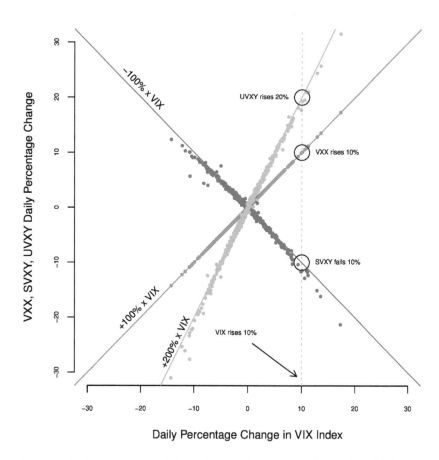

Figure 3.10: Daily returns of three VIX ETPs: VXX (unlevered), UVXY (2x levered) and SVXY (short volatility). Daily returns from October 2011 to September 2012. Source: Bloomberg.

Volatility in the form of VIX futures is an example of a market that was previously only within reach of large institutional investors such as hedge funds, pension and insurance companies. However in some markets exchange traded products have been so successful and have generated so much trading volume that markets start to be driven by ETP trading.

ETPs can generally be traded intra-day and so investors can rush to buy or sell at any time. Behind the scenes the issuer of the ETP will be buying or selling the underlying asset to match the shares outstanding in the ETP. Having a liquid ETP and an illiquid underlying creates a problem: a *liquidity mismatch*. If the ETP issuer cannot buy and sell the underlying as quickly as its own shares are bought and sold, then the returns of the ETP may start to deviate significantly from the underlying asset. The tracking error may then blow out.

The tracking error is usually small for ETPs that track the most liquid markets that have the most trading volume. Remember that the VIX futures market becomes more illiquid the longer the maturity. One-month VIX futures are much more liquid than two-month, and beyond seven months there is very little liquidity at all. If there is one very large participant in a small market then they will start to move the market. As they buy, the price will rise sharply and as they sell, the market will fall sharply. If a market participant becomes too big, they have difficulty finding enough buyers when they want to sell and enough sellers when they want to buy.

In Figure 3.11 we can see the tracking error for four VIX ETPs that in some way track the S&P short-term VIX futures index. VXX simply tracks the index with no leverage, SVXY is short the index with leverage -1, UVXY and TVIX are long the index with 2 times leverage. As you can see in the graphs, most of the time tracking error is very small, usually less than 1%. However on March 23rd 2012 the average weekly tracking error of TVIX blew out to about 20%. As the TVIX ETP grew in popularity it came to dominate the VIX futures market. By tracking the market it was itself distorting the market. The tracking error of VXX, which simply tracks the index with no leverage, and SVXY, which is short the index, are much smaller, seldom reaching 5%. UVXY is also two times levered, and although it tends to have a large tracking error this is nothing like that of TVIX.

The largest tracking error for TVIX occurred in March 2012. On February 21st the ETN issuer Credit Suisse announced that it would not issue any more TVIX units due to "internal limits". This probably means that so many people had bought the ETN that the risk of hedging the TVIX position in the VIX futures and derivatives market had grown too large. The demand for the ETN

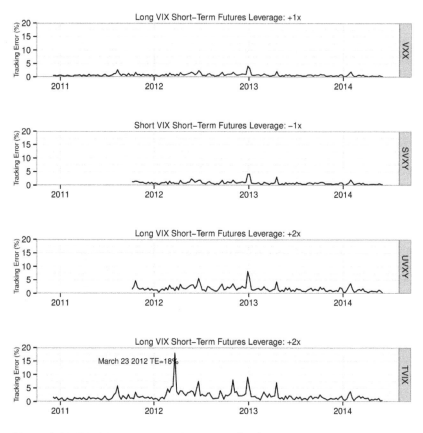

Figure 3.11: Weekly average tracking error for four VIX ETPs. Ideally tracking error should be zero, but in March 2012 tracking error for
TVIX increased significantly. Source: Bloomberg.

outstripped supply and the value rose far above its "fair value" (or net asset value in the language of exchange traded products). At one point the premium to its fair net asset value grew to around 80%. On March 22nd Credit Suisse announced that it would resume creation of new TVIX units and this coincides with the blow-out in tracking error as the price tumbled back down to its fair value. To quote from the Credit Suisse press release:[5]

> "As disclosed in the pricing supplement relating to the ETNs under the heading "Risk Factors—The Market Price of Your ETNs May Be Influenced By Many Unpredictable Factors," the market value of the ETNs may be influenced by, amongst other things, the levels of supply and demand for the ETNs. It is possible that the reopening of the ETNs on a limited basis, as described above, may influence the market value of the ETNs.

> Credit Suisse cannot predict with certainty what impact, if any, the reopening described above will have on the public trading price of the ETNs. It is possible that the resumption of new issuances of the ETNs, even on a limited basis, could reduce or remove any premium in the trading price of the ETNs over their indicative value. Investors are cautioned that paying a premium purchase price over the indicative value of the ETNs could lead to significant losses in the event the investor sells such ETNs at a time when the premium is no longer present in the market place or the ETNs are accelerated (including at our option), in which case investors will receive a cash payment in an amount equal to the closing indicative value on the accelerated valuation date."

If you read the documentation you will find that ETNs usually allow the issuer to stop issuing new units whenever they like, or to close the ETN and reimburse you with the fair value of the note whenever they like. If they stop issuing new units the price of the ETN will probably rise, but be aware that if the issuer chooses to start issuing units again, the premium will disappear and the price will fall sharply to its fair value. Another key point is that VIX exchange traded products with leverage tend to have larger tracking errors, extremely high volatility and, unless you have deep knowledge of the market, are probably best left to the professionals.

The market for volatility exchange traded products is fairly new and dynamic. Some ETPs may not last over the long-term due to a lack of popularity. Over the course of writing this book several new ETPs were created and several were withdrawn. If an ETP you own is withdrawn you will be given notice by your broker and will have time to sell into an orderly market and so this is not a calamity. But you should be aware that a lack of popularity makes it more likely that the issuer will decide to withdraw the ETP, so it is worth looking at the total assets or the net asset value of the ETP. Figure 3.12 shows the total assets of the largest volatility ETPs and how these have changed over the last four years. At the time of writing (2014) the largest VIX ETP is iPath's VIX Short-Term Futures ETN, ticker VXX, which has about $1 billion in total

---

[5]http://www.sec.gov/Archives/edgar/data/1053092/000095010312001467/
dp29470_fwp-tvix.htm

assets and has existed since 2009. For comparison the largest share ETF is SPY which has existed since 1993 and has over $120 billion in total assets.

Some exchange traded notes have a price at which they are automatically redeemed. For example VZZ (the S&P 500 VIX Mid-Term Futures ETN) was issued at a price of $30 but as volatility remained low its price rapidly fell in July 2011 to a value of $10 which was its automatic termination value. Holders of this note would have been repaid its redemption value of $10. A new ETN was issued with ticker VZZB and with the same name with the Roman numeral "II" appended to the name: "iPath Long Enhanced S&P 500 VIX Mid-Term Futures ETN" became "iPath Long Enhanced S&P 500 VIX Mid-Term Futures ETN (II)". This new note, issued at a price of $30, also had an automatic termination value of $10 which was reached, and the note was redeemed on October 5th 2012. As the documentation for VZZ said:

> Automatic Termination Event: We will automatically redeem your ETNs (in whole only, but not in part) if, on any valuation date prior to or on the final valuation date, the intraday indicative note value is less than or equal to 33.33% of the principal amount per ETN, or $10.00 for each ETN. We will redeem your ETNs on the automatic redemption date and will deliver a notice of redemption to The Depository Trust Company ("DTC") in the form attached as Annex C that will specify such date. Upon such redemption, you will receive a cash payment equal to the automatic redemption value. If periods of low market volatility occur during the term of your ETNs, the level of the Index may decrease at a precipitous rate, which may result in the triggering of an automatic termination event.

Note that automatic termination may also occur if volatility falls at a "precipitous rate" but this rate is never defined and is at the discretion of the ETN issuer. This fate also befell the IVO ETN (iPath Inverse S&P 500 VIX Short-Term Futures) which was redeemed and a new equivalent was issued with ticker IVOP and a "II" appended to its name.

The VIX ETP family

We can summarize the family of VIX exchange traded products as shown in Figure 3.13. The tickers are grouped according to whether they are based on short-term or mid-term VIX futures, whether they are levered, inverse or

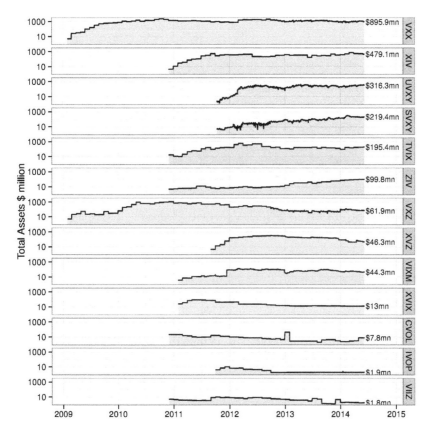

Figure 3.12: Total assets for the most popular VIX exchange traded products (logarithmic scale). Source: Bloomberg.

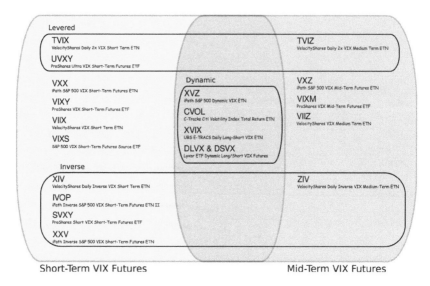

Figure 3.13: VIX exchange traded products grouped by the type of volatility index that they track.

dynamic/enhanced. Some ETPs are both levered and sensitive to short-term (TVIX and UVXY) or mid-term VIX futures (TVIZ). Inverse ETPs which are short VIX futures are also subdivided into being short short-term (such as XIV) and short mid-term VIX futures (such as ZIV). The cut-off where VIX futures switch from being short-term to mid-term is 4 months, such that 4-month up to 9-month VIX futures are considered mid-term. Dynamic, or enhanced VIX ETPs, are somewhat out on a limb because they are composed of a combination of long/short short-term and mid-term VIX futures. Having read this paragraph you will see why it is best to look at a diagram!

The majority of VIX exchange traded products are exchange traded notes, but a handful are exchange traded funds. This is an important distinction, because exchange traded funds carry no credit risk. In other words, if the ETF managing company goes bankrupt, the ETF investor's assets are not affected, as they are the owners of the assets in the fund, and another management company can take over running the fund. In the tables that follow you can see the ticker, fund manager, the annual fee they charge and the market capitalization of the fund as reported in 2014. The table is sorted by the size of the fund so you can quickly see the biggest funds. Generally the bigger the fund the better

Ticker	Name	Manager	Domicile	Fee	Assets $mn
UVXY	Ultra VIX Short-Term Futures	ProShares	US	0.95%	316.34
SVXY	Short VIX Short-Term Futures	ProShares	US	0.95%	219.42
VIXY	VIX Short-Term Futures	ProShares	US	0.85%	105.35
VIXM	VIX Mid-Term Futures	ProShares	US	0.85%	44.26
LVX	S&P 500 VIX Futures Enhanced Roll	Lyxor	France	0.60%	35.56
VIXS	S&P 500 VIX Short-Term Futures	Source	Ireland	0.60%	8.52
VIXH	CBOE S&P 500 VIX Tail Hedge Fund	First Trust	US	0.60%	5.91

Table 3.3: VIX dollar-denominated exchange traded funds. Source: Bloomberg.

as it should have a smaller bid-offer spread reducing your trading costs. And of course you would prefer fees to be as small as possible.

VIX exchange traded notes are more numerous than VIX exchange traded funds. Recall that when you buy exchange traded notes you are helping to fund the management company because the cash you pay and the assets that they buy are the property of the ETN issuer. This means that as an ETN investor you do not own the fund assets and should be concerned about the credit risk of the ETN issuer. If the issuer looks like it is in trouble financially, and its risk of default and bankruptcy increases, the value of the ETNs issued by that company will fall irrespective of the value of the assets in the fund. Again the table is sorted by the net asset value of the fund (in 2014) so that you can get an idea of the larger funds.

European volatility

VIX is a measure of volatility of stocks in the S&P 500 which is a US stock index. Investors in Europe can buy ETPs denominated in euro which are linked to the level of VIX. In addition to the risk of owning VIX these European investors are also exposed to currency risk, also called FX risk. As the value of the euro versus the dollar fluctuates, so will the value of euro-denominated VIX ETPs. In other words European investors in these products are making an investment in both volatility and the foreign exchange market.

For European investors the more natural hedge for their European stocks is to purchase exchange traded products that are related to the volatility of the Eurostoxx index or the German DAX index. The Eurostoxx volatility index

Ticker	Name	Manager	Fee	Assets $mn
VXX	S&P 500 VIX Short-Term Futures	Barclays iPath	0.89%	895.91
XIV	Daily Inverse VIX Short Term	VelocityShares	1.35%	479.06
TVIX	Daily 2x VIX Short Term	VelocityShares	1.65%	195.37
ZIV	Daily Inverse VIX Medium Term	VelocityShares	1.35%	99.75
VXZ	S&P 500 VIX Mid-Term Futures	Barclays iPath	0.89%	61.95
XVZ	S&P 500 Dynamic VIX	Barclays iPath	0.95%	46.26
XVIX	Daily Long-Short VIX	UBS E-TRACS	0.85%	13.02
VIIX	VIX Short Term	VelocityShares	0.89%	7.63
XXV	Inverse S&P 500 VIX Short-Term Futures	Barclays iPath	0.89%	3.71
IVOP	Inverse S&P 500 VIX Short-Term Futures II	Barclays iPath	0.89%	1.92
VIIZ	VIX Medium Term	VelocityShares	0.89%	1.75
TVIZ	Daily 2x VIX Medium Term	VelocityShares	1.65%	1.41

Table 3.4: VIX dollar-denominated exchange traded notes.   Source: Bloomberg.

Ticker	Name	Manager	Fee
VXIS	S&P 500 VIX Short-Term Futures ETN	Barclays iPath	-
VXIM	S&P 500 VIX Mid-Term Futures ETN	Barclays iPath	0.89%
VIXS	S&P 500 VIX Short-Term Futures ETF	Source	0.6%
VOLT	Voltage Mid-Term Source ETF	Nomura	0.3%
LVO	S&P 500 VIX Futures Enhanced Roll ETF	Lyxor	0.6%

Table 3.5: VIX euro-denominated exchange traded products.   Source: Bloomberg.

Ticker	Name	Manager	Fee
VSXX	VSTOXX Short-Term Futures Total Return ETN	Barclays iPath	-
VSXY	VSTOXX Mid-Term Futures Total Return ETN	Barclays iPath	0.89%

Table 3.6: VSTOXX euro-denominated exchange traded notes.   Source: Bloomberg.

is VSTOXX and the German volatility index is VDAX. The same principles apply to European volatility ETPs that apply to their US counterparts. Just as VIX ETPs depend on the VIX futures market, so VSTOXX ETPs depend on the futures market for VSTOXX. This means that all of the considerations about roll cost also apply to VSTOXX ETPs. For example there is a VSTOXX short-term futures index, a VSTOXX mid-term futures index, and even a dynamic VSTOXX index designed to give VSTOXX sensitivity without too great a roll cost. VSTOXX ETPs track these indices rather than VSTOXX directly. In the UK there are just two VIX ETNs which are currently available on the London Stock Exchange which trade in sterling: these are iPath's VXIS and VXIM. Unfortunately short volatility and dynamic VIX exchange traded products are not available in the UK at the time of writing.

Summary

Exchange traded products These are shares that trade on the stock market which can be linked to the value of anything, including volatility but also share indices, bond indices, and commodity prices like the price of gold and oil. Because they are shares they are liquid, which means you can buy and sell them quickly while markets are open with relatively small transaction costs.

Difference between ETF and ETN In an exchange traded fund (ETF) you own the assets bought by the fund manager. If the manager goes into bankruptcy you will not lose money and another manager will take over the fund. With an exchange traded note (ETN) the issuer owns the assets and you are lending the issuer your money. If the issuer becomes bankrupt you will lose a substantial amount of your capital. ETNs carry *credit risk* whereas ETFs do not.

ETP benefits ETPs create liquidity, which means that they take assets that

are hard for small investors to buy and sell and put these into investments that are easily bought and sold just like shares. They also provide
access to markets that small investors could not buy directly such as
international stock markets, commodities, and volatility.

ETP drawbacks The fund manager expects a fee. These can range from
0.4% per year to 1.5% per year of your investment for VIX ETPs, which
means for each $100 you invest you will pay up to $1.50 per year in fees.
ETPs are designed to track an index but fail to do so perfectly, and this
is tracking error. If tracking error is very high this calls into question
why you bought the ETP in the first place.

Short-term and mid-term ETPs There is a tradeoff between roll cost and
VIX sensitivity. Greater VIX sensitivity (percentage profit for a percentage rise in VIX) means greater roll cost. ETPs that track short-term VIX
futures have greater sensitivity and higher roll cost than mid-term VIX
futures.

Dynamic VIX futures index To appeal to retail investors S&P created this
index to (i) reduce volatility, which is closer to that of a bond than a
share, (ii) reduce roll cost. This index changes its allocation to short-
term and mid-term VIX futures according to the term structure of the
VIX futures curve. Again this comes at the price of reduced sensitivity
to VIX.

Short volatility and levered volatility Instead of buying volatility you can
sell volatility. When markets are quiet volatility falls and you can profit
from this fall by selling protection and going short VIX futures. This
is very risky because a short position in volatility during a stock market
crash will generate a severe loss. It is also possible to earn twice the
daily return from VIX (levered volatility) but again this is ultra-risky
and not advisable unless you are an expert.

VIX ETP Family This is the list of exchange traded products linked to volatility that you can trade. We can classify VIX exchang traded products
according to whether they are short-term (tickers VXX, VIXY, VIIX,
VIXS), mid-term (VXZ, VIXM, VIIZ) or dynamic (XVZ, CVOL, XVIX,
LVIX).

European volatility European investors have the choice of buying VIX exposure with an additional currency risk (tickers VIXS, VOLT and LYMJ)

---

or alternatively can invest in the home-grown European VSTOXX volatility index (VXIS for short-term and VXIM for mid-term).

4 Volatility trading strategies

At first, I was afraid, I was petrified
Kept thinking, I could never live without you by my side
But then I spent so many nights thinking how you did me wrong
And I grew strong, and I learned how to get along

Gloria Gaynor - I Will Survive

A trading strategy is a rule of thumb that tells you when to buy or sell an asset. In this final chapter I will suggest some strategies that have worked in the past. However take these with a large pinch of salt, because the future never *quite* resembles the past, so there is no guarantee that these strategies will work in future. These should be a starting point for you to develop your understanding of VIX and learn how to trade it profitably. No doubt you will come up with strategies of your own that suit your own investment style. The strategies will start simple and get a little bit more complex as the chapter progresses. But don't worry, this isn't a book for mathematicians, so I've deliberately kept the strategies very simple—as long as you can count you should be able to use them.

As we have already seen, volatility is special. Unlike the S&P 500, which can drift to any value and has no anchor, VIX is *mean-reverting*. Just as children return to mama, VIX always returns to its long-term average of 20%. Although you know as a certainty that VIX will revert to its mean, you do not know when this will happen. The simplest strategy would seem to be to buy VIX when it is below 20% and sell VIX when it is above 20%. In the real world you have to choose how to get long or short VIX exposure, and this critically affects your strategy. Exchange traded products like VXX and VXZ have a punitive cost of carry which will haemorrhage your capital unless VIX rises quickly. So you have to be right, and right quickly, if you choose to go long VIX with these products.

If you are willing to wait a bit longer and make less profit if you are right, then buying VIX when it is cheap is best achieved through dynamic VIX products such as XVZ that reduce the roll cost. Going short VIX through products like SVXY you can afford to be more relaxed about timing because roll is to your advantage, although you could make severe losses if a crisis occurs when you are short volatility. Even being short VIX does not completely avoid roll cost worries because if you are holding your short position once VIX is above around 31% then the volatility term structure will probably invert and you will be losing money through roll. Carry matters very much to *all* VIX exchange traded products so skip back to Section "What is roll cost?" if you aren't sure about the nature of carry and roll cost.

Risk and return

When investing a good place to start is to consider past risk and return. If you are taking a greater risk of losing your invested capital you deserve a greater average return. In Table 4.1 we can see the risk and return for one-month to six-month VIX futures. These UBS ETRACS exchange traded notes were issued in September 2011 and later withdrawn in 2012. However they provide a beautiful illustration that carry cost is greater for shorter-dated VIX futures. VXAA gave exposure to the one-month VIX future and had the biggest loss (75%), and VXFF which gave exposure to the six-month VIX future, had the smallest loss (31%). The volatility, or risk, of these products also varied smoothly with the term of the VIX future. Short-dated VIX futures are more risky than long-dated VIX futures. VXAA had an annual volatility of 72%, whereas VXFF had a volatility of just 30%. Remember that an average stock has a volatility of about 30%.

What this means for an investor is that any strategy that is exposed to the short-term part of the VIX futures curve (such as VXX) will be more risky than the long-term part of the curve (VXZ). And we also have to consider carry costs because the steep short-dated part of the VIX futures curve is expensive to hold over the long term.

We compare several other exchange traded products in the same way in Figure 4.1. However it is important to note that VIX ETPs are a fairly recent arrival to the ETP fold and so many products have not been around very long. The return and volatility in Figure 4.1 is over the life of the product, which is also shown. The table is sorted in order of increasing risk. The least risky VIX ETPs are XVIX and XVZ, which are the dynamic VIX products that are designed to reduce carry cost and volatility. In terms of volatility these ETPs look more like bonds than stocks with volatility less than the average stock but notice that they were issued after the Credit Crisis. If they had been issued in 2006, their lifetime volatility would definitely be closer to the S&P Dynamic VIX index (SPDVIXTR in the table), which publishes returns back to the end

Ticker	Term	Return	Volatility
VXFF	6-Month S&P 500 VIX Futures	-30.5	29.6
VXEE	5-Month S&P 500 VIX Futures	-38.8	39.0
VXDD	4-Month S&P 500 VIX Futures	-46.4	40.8
VXCC	3-Month S&P 500 VIX Futures	-51.6	44.8
VXBB	2-Month S&P 500 VIX Futures	-63.2	60.2
VXAA	1-Month S&P 500 VIX Futures	-74.5	72.1

Table 4.1: Comparison of return and volatility for UBS ETRACS VIX exchange traded notes (September 2011 to November 2012). Source: Bloomberg.

of 2005 and has a volatility of 26% over this period.

Mid-term VIX futures products are next in the risk spectrum and cluster around the VIX mid-term futures index (SPVXMTR) with a stock-like volatility since 2005 of 33%. More risky still are short-term VIX futures ETPs and the S&P short-term VIX futures index itself with a volatility of 63%. VIX has an extremely high volatility of 98% since it was first published in 1990. Finally at the riskiest end of the spectrum are levered products such as TVIX (volatility 134%) and UVXY (volatility 146%), which are both designed to give exposure to two times levered VIX short term futures.

Looking at the returns in Figure 4.1, the products that simply track parts of the VIX futures curve obviously have a negative return over their lifetime. However short volatility VIX products which sell volatility have clearly performed well recently. For example XXV (iPath Inverse S&P 500 VIX Short-Term Futures) had a large annual return of 20% and a low volatility of just 12% over its three and a half year lifetime.

Strategy 1: Switch between dynamic VIX and shares

As we have seen VIX and the stock market usually move in opposite directions. We have also seen that VIX tends to be sticky, such that once it is high it stays high. For example see Figure 1.14 which shows that, on average, it has taken over 200 days for VIX to return to 20% if it was at 40%. Our first strategy takes advantage of this behaviour by having a crisis switch. When volatility is high stocks tend to perform poorly and dynamic VIX performs well, so the strategy sells its shares and buys dynamic VIX. When the crisis passes the strategy sells its dynamic VIX exposure and buys stocks. If this

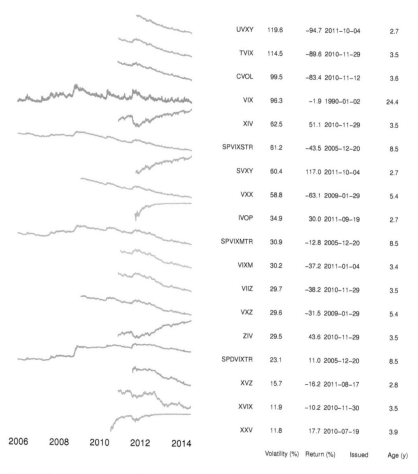

	Volatility (%)	Return (%)	Issued	Age (y)
UVXY	119.6	−94.7	2011−10−04	2.7
TVIX	114.5	−89.6	2010−11−29	3.5
CVOL	99.5	−83.4	2010−11−12	3.6
VIX	96.3	−1.9	1990−01−02	24.4
XIV	62.5	51.1	2010−11−29	3.5
SPVIXSTR	61.2	−43.5	2005−12−20	8.5
SVXY	60.4	117.0	2011−10−04	2.7
VXX	58.8	−63.1	2009−01−29	5.4
IVOP	34.9	30.0	2011−09−19	2.7
SPVIXMTR	30.9	−12.8	2005−12−20	8.5
VIXM	30.2	−37.2	2011−01−04	3.4
VIIZ	29.7	−38.2	2010−11−29	3.5
VXZ	29.6	−31.5	2009−01−29	5.4
ZIV	29.5	43.6	2010−11−29	3.5
SPDVIXTR	23.1	11.0	2005−12−20	8.5
XVZ	15.7	−16.2	2011−08−17	2.8
XVIX	11.9	−10.2	2010−11−30	3.5
XXV	11.8	17.7	2010−07−19	3.9

Figure 4.1: Comparison of return and volatility for VIX exchange traded products and the S&P short-term (SPVXSTR), mid-term (SPVXMTR) and dynamic (SPDVIXTR) VIX futures indices. Products are sorted in descending order of volatility. Source: Bloomberg.

strategy works it will benefit during crises as volatility rises and benefit from stock market rallies between crises. The strategy shows that:

The "best" strategy is continually changing Dynamic VIX has only been around for a short time so the strategy is still learning from experience. The shock-rich period from 2006 to 2014 is likely to be too disaster-prone to be representative of the long-term.

Dynamic VIX was hard to beat (2006-2012) Dynamic VIX was better than the strategy until 2013 when the strategy pulled ahead. This year marks the point when the succession of global financial crises started to subside. Stocks had been rallying since 2009 but this rally came with high volatility. In 2013 the S&P 500 rallied strongly and volatility fell back to very low levels, mostly below 20% so that dynamic VIX started to fall behind stocks.

Trading costs matter I have assumed a 1% trading cost (if you buy $100 worth of ETP you will lose a dollar each time you trade). Don't over-trade or you will eat away at your investment! Incorporating a trading cost means the strategy will trade as infrequently as possible.

The strategy is designed to be very simple. On any day you will either be fully invested in dynamic VIX or the S&P 500. You simply look back over a "window" of 6 trading days. Then count how many consecutive days VIX has been above a threshold value of 17.4%. If VIX is above this level for 6 consecutive days you buy a dynamic VIX ETP (such as XVZ). If VIX closes below 17.4% on any day in your "window" you sell your dynamic VIX ETF and buy an S&P 500 ETF (such as SPY).

If VIX > 17.4% for 6 consecutive days

>**Buy** your S&P dynamic VIX index[a]

>**Sell** your S&P 500 shares ETP[b]

Otherwise

>**Buy** your S&P 500 shares ETP

>**Sell** your S&P dynamic VIX ETP

---

[a]Such as XVZ.
[b]Such as SPY.

We will look to see whether this strategy made money in the past. The critical question is: what is the best size of the look-back "window" and the threshold value of VIX? The values above are tuned to generate the most profit based on data since 2006 with a 1% trading cost. Unfortunately the dynamic VIX index, which is published by Standard and Poor's and tracked by exchange traded products like XVZ, has only been calculated since 2006. The reason why this is a problem is that the eight years from 2006 to 2014 have been unusually volatile, spanning two global financial crises. Looking back further there have been multi-year periods of very low volatility when our strategy that is tuned for the disaster-prone period of 2006-2014 would perform poorly because it would spend too little time invested in stocks.

With the caveat about the short history of the dynamic VIX index in mind we can look at the how the optimal window and threshold for buying the index differed in the past. Our test must use a very important rule: *never use information from the future*. Of course we know all about the Credit Crisis now so we can tune our VIX threshold to take this into account. But when testing our strategy it could not have known about the size of the crisis beforehand. I have broken down the period since 2006 into annual periods and the strategy sees one new year at a time and is tested on volatility performance for the next year about which it is "ignorant".

Our test begins in 2007. All our strategy is allowed to see is a history of volatility over 2006 and sets its parameters using this single year's data and uses them to trade during 2007. The average value of VIX was just 12.8% in 2006 so we might expect that the threshold will be a little above this average. Note that the longer the look-back "window" and the greater the difference between the VIX threshold and the average level of VIX the less often the strategy trades and the less money it loses in trading costs. It turns out that the strategy is is indeed choosing to trade very infrequently: the best threshold of 16.5% was well above the 2006 VIX average with a window of 5 days. Based on a "memory" of 2006, in 2007 the strategy was invested in stocks in the first half of the year and switched to dynamic VIX in the second half as VIX rose above the threshold of 16.5% in July and stayed there. The first test period (2007) gave a return for the strategy of 22% which was a lot better than the S&P (3%) but not quite as good as the dynamic VIX index (26%).

Figure 4.2 shows the results as we increase the market memory of the strategy year by year. The top panel shows the cumulative value of $100 invested at the beginning of 2006 in the strategy or in the dynamic VIX or the S&P 500 ETF (SPY) indices. By the last test period in 2014 the strategy can draw on the full eight year experience of how volatility and stocks behaved between 2006 and 2014. The dynamic strategy outperforms eventually but only in 2013 when dynamic VIX started to significantly and consistently under-perform the

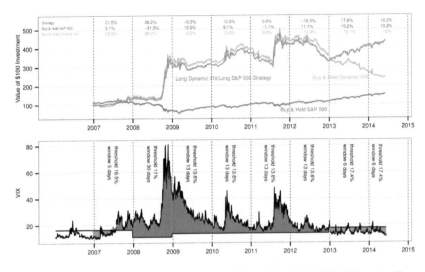

Strategy	21.5%	88.2%	−0.2%	12.6%	9.8%	−16.3%	17.8%	10.2%
Buy & Hold S&P 500	3.1%	−31.5%	19.5%	8.1%	−1.1%	11.1%	19.2%	10.2%
Buy & Hold Dynamic VIX	25.0%	88.2%	−0.2%	12.6%	9.8%	13.9%	18.1%	11%

Figure 4.2: Switching between dynamic VIX and the S&P 500. Blue shading indicates when the strategy is invested in the dynamic VIX index, red when invested in the S&P 500. Source: Bloomberg.

S&P 500.

The strategy had its best return of 88% during 2008. Given its memory of 2006-2007 the optimal window and VIX threshold were 30 days and 11.0%. Because VIX was very high throughout 2008 the strategy was invested in dynamic VIX for the entire 2008 period and earned a return of 88.2%. In 2009 the strategy goes badly wrong. The best strategy was to buy stock for this year as stocks rallied by 19.5% and dynamic VIX was flat but the three-year old strategy, little more than a toddler, was still in shock from record levels of VIX seen in 2008. In fact the best threshold and window was stuck at a threshold that always went long dynamic VIX for the next four years (a very low threshold of 13.6% and a window of 13 days) during the volatility aftershocks of the flash crash and sovereign debt crisis in 2010 and the debt ceiling crash of August 2011.

Overall the strategy returned 15.3% annually which beat the simple act of buying and holding dynamic VIX in 2006 which returned an overall annual 11.4%. The reason why this out-performance is small is that dynamic VIX is good at its job. It does not lose much value due to roll cost, which is the whole point of its being dynamic. One of the attractions of the dynamic VIX index is that it has low volatility compared with VIX itself or the short-term and mid-term VIX futures indices (see Figure 4.1). The dynamic VIX index has an annualized daily volatility of 23.3% from its inception in December 2005 until January 2014. This is comparable with the volatility risk of a stock in a large and established company. Since 1990 VIX has had a daily volatility of 96% which is four times as risky.

The take-home here is clear: dynamic VIX is usually good for profiting from volatility gains while not losing a lot in roll cost. Dynamic VIX gives you less boost in value than a short-term VIX futures product when vol does shoot up, but that insensitivity is the price you pay for less roll cost. A strategy laid on top of dynamic VIX to tell you when to buy and sell will not boost your return much but is probably still worthwhile if we are entering a new phase of calm markets where stocks will prosper. However dynamic VIX is still not a buy and hold investment because if crises fail to materialize it will not gain in value. This is the kind of product you have to actively manage. Dynamic VIX will work best if you keep an eye on the news for the type of event that will wake the volatility dragon. If you don't want to scour the news daily you can use something like the simple rule above to detect when the volatility dragon stirs.

Strategy 2: Long/Short Short-term VIX Futures

Our next strategy is more risky but potentially also much more profitable. It is more risky because it uses the short-term futures index which is more volatile than dynamic VIX, is more sensitive to VIX movements and has a very large roll cost. The idea is that you go long short-term VIX futures while volatility is high and short short-term VIX futures while volatility is low. This means that you can make money as vol moves up and as vol moves down, and also profit from roll while volatility is low.

Again we use our simple method of counting days when VIX is above some threshold as a trading signal. This time the "best" strategy tuned to the extremely volatile last six years is as follows:

> **If** VIX closed above 24.8% on the last trading day
>
>> **Buy** your **long** S&P short-term VIX futures ETP[a]
>>
>> **Sell** your short S&P short-term VIX futures ETP[b]
>
> **otherwise** if VIX closed below 24.8% on the last trading day
>
>> **Buy** your **short** S&P short-term VIX futures ETP
>>
>> **Sell** your long S&P short-term VIX futures ETP
>
> ---
> [a]Such as VXX, VIXY, VIIX or VIXS.
> [b]Such as XIV, IVOP, SVXY or XXV.

You will always have either positive or negative exposure to VIX with this strategy. At any time you will own either a long VIX ETP (like VXX) or short VIX ETP (like SVXY). Notice that the window for this strategy is just one day, which is much shorter than the dynamic VIX strategy. That is because the price of short-term VIX futures products move much more rapidly and violently than medium-term VIX futures products so you can't afford to react slowly. Consequently the strategy always sets a VIX threshold that is very high or very low to avoid trading too much and eroding any gains with trading costs. This means the strategy must either be biased to be long volatility with a preference to buy VXX or short volatility when the preference switches to SVXY.

The top panel in Figure 4.3 shows the cumulative return of a dollar invested in either the long-short strategy or a short short-term VIX futures ETP at the end of 2005. Notice that the vertical axis is logarithmic so the value of that $100 investment increased more than seven-hundred-fold over this period of eight years, with an average annual return of 103% while a short short-term VIX strategy was much more modest (annualized return was 9%) and the over-all S&P annualized return was just 2.6%. The bottom pane shows the level of VIX with shading relative to the level of the threshold and the colour of the shading indicates whether the strategy is long volatility or short volatility.

The overall returns with this strategy are much higher and much more volatile than the dynamic VIX strategy. However because this strategy always has a shorter VIX window it is buying and selling more often than the dynamic VIX strategy the cost of trading has a much bigger impact on profit. For this anal-ysis I have assumed a huge trading cost of 1% difference (spread) in buying (offer) and selling (bid) price. In practice, at the time of writing in 2014, the bid-offer spread on VXX is at least ten times smaller than this, but in some countries investors have to pay a trading tax so you may have to factor in a higher trading cost even though bid-offer spread is tight.

As for the first strategy I have optimized the strategy cumulatively in six month periods to show how a pre-credit-crisis view of the World was fundamentally altered after the Lehman default. The results are shown in Figure 4.3. Initially the model only "knows" data from December 2005 to June 2006 and over this period it was best to have no window at all and to react to raw VIX on a daily basis. Also note that the VIX threshold is just 16.0% so the strategy would go long short-term volatility if VIX was above 16% and short otherwise. This actually works well during the test period of July to December 2006 generating a return of over 100%. During the first half of 2007 the strategy has six months more experience and raises the threshold slightly to 16.5%. During the second half of 2007 as the Credit Crisis starts to unfold VIX rises above the threshold of 16.5% and remains there for the rest of 2007, so the strategy is short volatility until July then long until December and this works very well indeed.

In 2008 and 2009 the strategy is always long volatility which generates a very high return in 2008 but is disastrous in 2009 when VIX peaks at around 60% in spring then collapses back toward its long-term average of 20%. Because we prevent the model from seeing the future it has never experienced a 2009 volatility collapse and so is not capable of dealing with it. However by July 2010 the strategy has learned from the 2009 volatility collapse and decides it is safe to be short volatility. The strategy returns to its preference to be short volatility by doubling its VIX threshold from 13.6% to 24.8% where it has remained ever since. After this change the strategy starts generating profits again and has performed well since the post-Lehman volatility crash. In 2011 the model was long volatility during spike in VIX between August and December as the US debt ceiling negotiations shocked markets. In 2012 the model was almost completely short as volatility was fairly benign except for a few days in summer.

Overall this strategy performed spectacularly well in five out of six years for which data are available, and spectacularly badly in 2009 and the first half of 2010. The volatility of the strategy returns is 64% which is very risky indeed, twice that of an average stock. This means that on average your investment is very likely to fall by 64% in one year or rise 64% in one year which puts it into the realms of speculation rather than investment. However for those who have a voracious appetite for risk this might be something to consider.

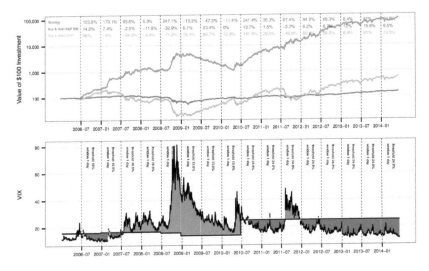

Figure 4.3: Long/short short-term VIX. Red shading indicates the strategy is long volatility, blue indicates short volatility. Source: Bloomberg.

Strategy 3: Incorporating Dynamic VIX into your portfolio

A more balanced approach to investing in volatility, and one that most people reading this are likely to consider, is including it into a balanced long-term portfolio. By balanced I mean that the portfolio has a wide variety of different investments which is universally agreed to be a Good Idea. This is because a disaster in one asset class is less likely to wipe out your capital as your eggs are in many baskets. Another reason is that day-to-day fluctuations in the value of your portfolio are damped down by having unrelated assets that are driven by different factors. Diversification is therefore one of the attributes of a well-constructed portfolio, in addition to the more obvious one of high return.

A shocking fact tends to make diversification difficult. The shocking fact is that every investible asset class is often highly correlated with other investible asset classes. If two assets are correlated this means that when one asset price rises or falls the other rises or falls in lock-step. To take an example if you have two technology stocks, such as Apple and Google, their share prices will rise and fall together. You either buy one or the other because either exposes you to a fundamental market driver which is "US technology company". If you have a dollar in Apple then investing a dollar in Google is just another dollar invested in "US technology company" because these two stocks are highly correlated. That extra dollar will not increase your percentage return and it will not decrease your portfolio volatility. However if you invest that dollar into a dynamic VIX exchange traded product (such as XVZ) you will almost certainly decrease your portfolio volatility. Don't believe me? Well, let's try it out.

We can start with an investor who just buys the S&P 500 and earns the capital return (increase in the price of the index) and the dividend on the stocks in the index. Then we can compare their historic portfolio return and volatility with that of an investor that invests in both dynamic VIX and the S&P 500. Finally we will add other, more traditional, assets to the mix and see which ETFs are most appropriate for the purpose of producing diversified returns.

In order to compare investments we need some kind of yardstick, and return is insufficient because it ignores the risk we took to generate that return. To construct this investment yardstick we will always subtract the return on US bank deposit rates from our asset returns because cash is the much lower risk and lower return alternative to putting your capital at risk in bond and stock markets. The return we end up with is then *excess return* above the (almost) risk-free cash rate. Dividing excess return by volatility gives us a risk-adjusted return, or Sharpe ratio, which tells us how much extra return we get for each unit of risk we take. Ideally we would like to have investments and portfolios that have a high return for a low risk. We want a large Sharpe ratio.

Portfolio Ingredients

The ingredients in our portfolio as measured by this risk-adjusted return yardstick for the period from the end of 2005 to mid-2014 are shown in Figure 4.4. The dynamic VIX index is best in terms of Sharpe ratio. The Sharpe ratio was the excess return divided by the volatility which is 6.7% / 23.9% which is 0.28. Note that SPDVIXTR is an index not an ETP so does not incorporate fees. Even if we subtract 1% annual fees the Sharpe ratio is still best at 0.24. Gold was next best with an equity-like volatility (22%) but a better return than equity (3.4%), and this gave a reasonable Sharpe ratio of 0.15. Fixed income had a low Sharpe ratio because of low return despite its very low volatility. The S&P 500 equity ETF (SPY) had the worst of both worlds, with low average annual excess return above cash of 2% due to the Credit Crisis crash and high volatility of 22% giving a Sharpe ratio of just 0.09. Note that the government bond ETF (SHY) had a negative excess return because during this period of record low rates government bond yields were close to the cash rate.

This means that their excess return (excess above the cash rate) was usually negative once ETF fees of 0.15% were deducted.

The portfolio ingredients respond quite differently to crises. If we look at the volatility of each of these five ingredients over the period since 2006 taking care to show them on the same scale then the difference becomes very clear, as shown in Figure 4.5. US Treasuries (SHY) have been a bastion of calm with a volatility of under 2%. Only a very slight blip registers after the default of Lehman Brothers as investors fled to the safety of US government debt. The Barclays bond aggregate also has a very low volatility of 5%, but contains corporate bonds which have a corporate credit risk which is bound to fall in value during a credit crisis. Ironically this used to be known as the Lehman aggregate index, but Barclays bought the rights to the index after the demise of Lehman. As its namesake collapsed the index remained fairly calm with volatility briefly topping 25%. Gold and the S&P 500 have very similar average volatility of around 20% and both became much more volatile during the Credit Crisis. The most panic-stricken ingredient is the dynamic VIX index, but importantly it *gained* value during these panics. If we want a safety net, or hedge, against falls in the stock market, dynamic VIX ticks this box over this period.

Bubble plots show average returns, but mask whether the asset price tends to crash, so in Figure 4.6 we can see these returns. The return for the portfolio ingredients in the period since 2006 shows that the best performer was the dynamic VIX index, with an overall return of about 8% each year. This is more than the return in the bubble plot because we have not subtracted the 1.1% cash rate, so the return numbers in Figure 4.6 are total returns not excess returns. This period was particularly volatile when compared with the last fifty years and so this is precisely the environment in which dynamic VIX would perform well. Most of the dynamic VIX index return comes from the two big volatility spikes in 2008 and 2011 and has been gradually falling during the low volatility period since 2012. This nicely illustrates the beautiful equity hedging properties of dynamic VIX: as the S&P 500 tumbles the dynamic VIX index, unlike bonds or gold, rallies to compensate. Gold, which performs well during financial crises, and in periods of low interest rates, was almost as good as dynamic VIX with a return of 5% each year. Shares unsurprisingly suffered from being a risky asset and were roughly flat with a return of just 3% each year but this period included the 52% Credit Crisis fall and post-crisis rally of over 100% that just compensated the loss. Fixed income plodded along with the Barclays Agg rising 2% and Treasuries creeping up by around 1% each year.

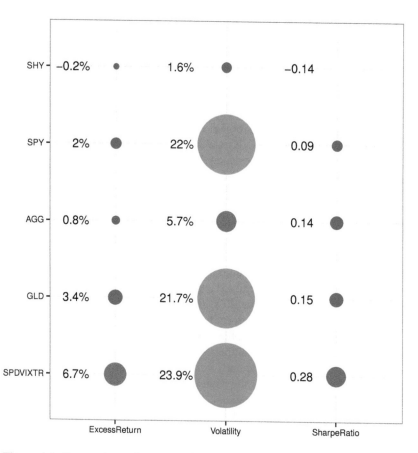

Figure 4.4: Comparison of return and volatility for US Treasuries (SHY), Barclays bond aggregate (AGG), S&P 500 (SPY) and the S&P dynamic VIX futures index (SPDVIXTR). Data are from Dec 2005 to June 2014. Source: Bloomberg.

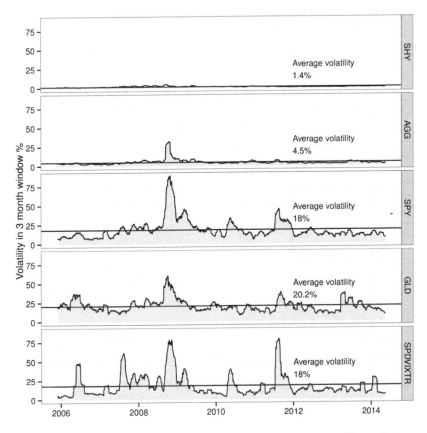

Figure 4.5: Volatility of portfolio ingredients over a 30-day rolling window (SHY tracks US Treasuries, AGG tracks the Barclays aggregate bond index, SPY tracks the S&P 500, GLD tracks gold and SPDVIXTR is the dynamic VIX index). Source: Bloomberg.

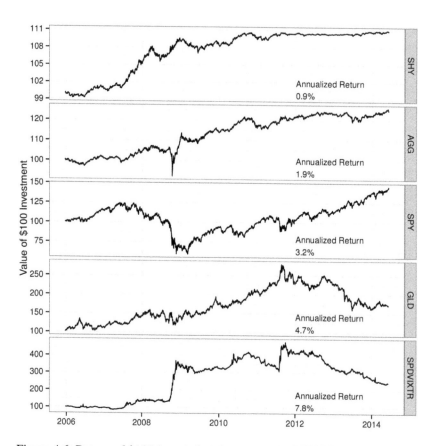

Figure 4.6: Return of $100 invested at the very end of 2005 in US Treasuries (SHY), the broad US bond market (AGG), the S&P 500 stock index (SPY), gold (GLD) and dynamic VIX (SPDVIXTR). Source: Bloomberg.

Combining the ingredients

Now we know the ingredients we can add them together. There is a way of working out the amount of each ingredient which combines two types of information to create a portfolio with the optimum risk-adjusted return: firstly it uses the risk-adjusted return of each asset individually (of course) and secondly it uses correlation between asset prices. If two assets have prices that move in opposite directions then when they are combined they will cancel out some volatility for the portfolio. Dynamic VIX is negatively correlated with stocks and so these two naturally form a pair that will "go well together". As S&P 500 share prices tumble VIX rises and as shares rise VIX falls. Using this maximum Sharpe ratio recipe we can see what the returns would have been as we add each ingredient.

Looking at the individual risk-adjusted returns in Figure 4.4 the best performer (risk-adjusted or not) over this volatile period is dynamic VIX. Consequently the biggest allocation, over half the portfolio, is invested in dynamic VIX (see Figure 4.7). In each row of Figure 4.7 we add one asset, starting with the S&P 500 ETF (SPY) alone, then adding dynamic VIX (SPDVIXTR), US Treasuries (SPY), gold (GLD) and the Barclays bond aggregate (AGG). In the top row the S&P alone gained 2.1% in excess of cash returns with volatility 22%. Adding dynamic VIX in the second row of Figure 4.7 doubled the return, halved the volatility, and increased the risk-adjusted return five-fold. Adding government bonds to the mix made little impact because shares and VIX were already paired up and diversified and government bonds have a low excess return. The negative Sharpe ratio of government bonds attracted almost no capital at all. In contrast gold performed well over this period, albeit with high volatility, and draws 11% of the allocation, increasing the overall return and reducing the portfolio volatility slightly. The Barclays Aggregate bond index tracker AGG received a fairly large allocation of around 31% because it provided some diversification.

The key message from Figure 4.7 is surprising. The conventional portfolio mix is 60% shares, 40% bonds with the justification that over the long-term bonds earn less than shares but they provide a hedge in case share prices crash. It turns out that the conventional portfolio now that VIX exchange traded products are available is quite different. The best mix over the 2006-2014 period would have been about equal amounts of shares, bonds and dynamic VIX. During volatile periods such as 2008-2011 a large allocation to dynamic VIX combined with a stock index performs very well with a fairly low risk. Remember that the volatility of the three primary ingredients were all around

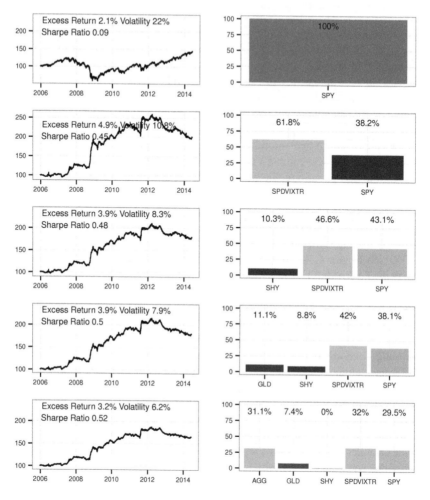

Figure 4.7: Graphs in the left column show return of $100 invested portfolios with the weights in the right column. The top row is returns of the S&P 500 ETF (SPY) alone, row two adds Dynamic VIX (SPDVIXTR), row three adds US Treasuries (SHY), row four adds gold (GLD), final row adds the Barclays bond aggregate (AGG). Returns and volatilities are annualized. Source: Bloomberg.

20% (S&P 500 22%, Dynamic VIX 24%, gold 22%) but the combined portfolio volatility was 7.2%. In other words by owning the "right" amount of each asset we created a portfolio with less than half the volatility of its ingredients. This is not magic: when stocks fall dynamic VIX rises. This is diversification in action. But you may be wondering why not put all your money into dynamic VIX and earn 6.7% excess return instead of 4.9% with stocks and dynamic VIX? The answer is that this is much riskier. Dynamic VIX had a good run during this period, but if we had chosen 2003 to 2007 when VIX was abnormally low for several years this gamble would have lost money, as equities outperformed. Putting all your money in one asset is gambling, not investment.

A very large allocation to dynamic VIX is unlikely to work in less crisis-prone environments. If we break down the returns for the two-asset portfolio into quarterly contributions from the S&P 500 and dynamic VIX we can see that the returns are dominated by two massive volatility rallies during Q3 2008 and Q2 2011 (see Figure 4.8). Unless ultra-high volatility and regular stock market crashes are the "new normal" it is likely that the best dynamic VIX allocation would be much lower than 50% and the best S&P 500 allocation will be higher than 25%. In the final Chapter we look at what the best VIX allocation might be in a less volatile future.

Summary

Trading strategy A trading strategy is a rule for deciding what to buy and sell and how to time your trade. The three strategies we discuss are examples and should be taken as a very rough guide because as conditions change the best rules change. You should use these examples to build your own strategies using back-testing. Find strategies that fit your investment style and risk appetite.

Strategy 1: Switch between dynamic VIX and shares This is for long-term investors that don't want too much risk. This strategy switches between dynamic VIX and the S&P 500. If VIX closes above 17.4% on six successive days the strategy buys dynamic VIX and the rest of the time the strategy buys the S&P 500.

Strategy 2: Long/Short Short-term VIX Futures A more risky strategy with much higher volatility than Strategy 1. If VIX closes above 24.8%

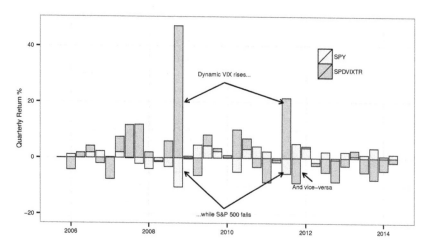

Figure 4.8: Quarterly return contributions for two-asset portfolio containing the S&P 500 ETF (SPY) and the Dynamic VIX Index
(SPDVIXTR). Source: Bloomberg.

you buy a short-term VIX futures ETP such as VXX. Otherwise you
short volatility with an ETP such as SVXY.

Strategy 3: Incorporating Dynamic VIX into your portfolio VIX will probably be an addition to existing assets in your portfolio. It turns out that
the best risk-adjusted return during the crisis-prone 2006-2014 period
was to have the following combination of assets: 32% dynamic VIX,
31% US bonds, 30% S&P 500, 7% gold and no Treasuries at all. This is
a far cry from the conventional 60% share 40% bond portfolio. If, like
me, you're not expecting another Credit Crisis with ultra-high volatility
then the dynamic VIX allocation looks too high and the share component too low. See the final Chapter on how to account for this.

5 The future

"One thing is that I can live with doubt and uncertainty and not knowing. I think it's much more interesting to live not knowing than to have answers which might be wrong."

Richard Feynman

While it is possible to draw lessons from the past as investors we are interested in the future. Unfortunately the period from 2006 to 2013 during which we have data for VIX total return indices has been exceptionally volatile with an armada of crises. Of course there will be global financial crises in future but it is important to remember that, despite recent history, in the long-run global financial crises do not happen very often. If we invest with a perpetual doom-laden viewpoint we will be guaranteed to lose money. After the second World War investors could be justified for thinking that one global war per generation was a natural state of affairs. Their fathers had fought in a global conflict, they themselves had fought in a global conflict, so surely their children would also have their own global conflict? But of course that did not happen, and after WWII there was a white-hot equity rally from 1950 to 1970.

Before looking to the future it pays to look deep into the past. Robert Shiller's S&P 500 monthly prices (which we used to study black swans in Figure 1.6) go all the way back to 1870 and this allows us to calculate monthly volatility stretching back 140 years (see Figure 5.1). I have also overlaid daily realized volatility for the S&P 500 going back to 1950 and of course VIX. Monthly data miss the sharp peaks that make or break a volatility trade so this graph is purely for comparison, but what is clear is that the Great Depression in the 1930s was by far the biggest volatility spike over the last century. In fact if we had daily data over this period it would exceed by far the peaks we saw in 1987 and 2008. The lessons we can draw from this long-term view are that volatility is not higher than it was in the past and recent crises are not more severe than those in the past.

What should we expect following the Credit Crisis and European sovereign debt crisis? Is it inevitable that we will see more frequent and more severe global crises? Personally I believe that the extreme volatility we saw in 2008

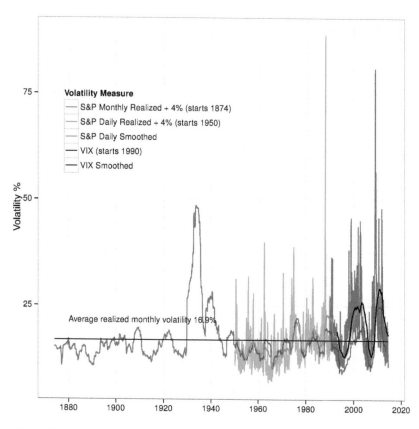

Figure 5.1: Long-term volatility comparing S&P monthly realized (starts 1870), S&P daily realized (starts 1950) and VIX (starts 1990). Volatility during the Great Depression dwarfs all other events in the last century including the Credit Crisis. Source: Bloomberg, Shiller.

will not be repeated in the coming decade. This means that all the trading strategies we developed in Chapter 3 will be tuned for another World War in volatility that will never materialize. Although we can't change the past it is possible to edit out the most extreme days. In this final Chapter we consider what would have happened if we snip out just the very worst and best few days over the 2006-2014 period. Wait, did you read that right, did I say *best*? In Section "Tail events" in Chapter 1 we saw that so-called black swans, very rare and awful negative returns, flock with golden swans, days of exceptionally high positive returns. So we are throwing away these exceptionally good and bad days and sticking to the humdrum daily grind of markets. This is by no means a perfect way of forecasting future volatility as there was a strong rally following the global financial crisis which may not have happened without the crisis itself.

The criterion I have chosen for "forgetting" a day is that VIX closed above 63.8%, which occurred just 1% of the time from 2006 to 2014. In fact the only years since 1990 in which VIX *ever* closed above 63.8% were 20 days in 2008. The results of editing these extremely volatile days are shown in Figure 5.2. Although forgetting 20 days may not seem significant the impact on equity returns and volatility returns is dramatic. Instead of falling 38.5% in 2008 the S&P 500 share index only fell 9%. The impact on dynamic VIX is more dramatic still: instead of a 139% return in 2008 the return was a mere 15%.

Now we turn to the effect of editing out the 20 most volatile days on our first strategy (see Figure 5.3). This switches between dynamic VIX and the S&P 500 according to the level of VIX. Previously we found that it was best to look back over a window of 6 days and if on any day VIX closed above 17.4% the strategy should buy dynamic VIX otherwise it should buy an S&P 500 ETF. The best window for the less crisis-prone history is much longer, 27 days, and the VIX threshold is now lower, 15.6% instead of 17.4%. A shorter window and lower threshold mean that the strategy is more likely to jump to crisis mode switching out of stocks into dynamic VIX.

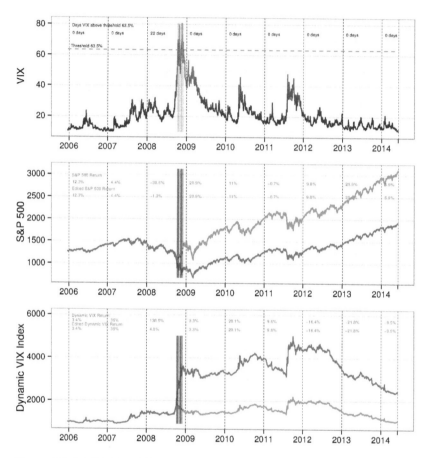

Figure 5.2: S&P 500 and Dynamic VIX returns with and without high volatility days (greater than 63.8%) removed. High volatility days highlighted with shading. Source: Bloomberg.

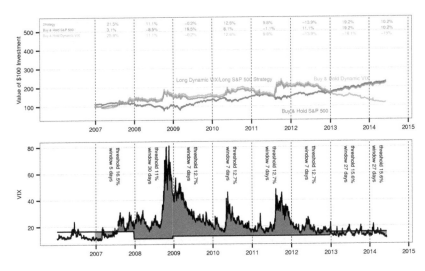

Figure 5.3: Switching between dynamic VIX and the S&P 500. Blue shading indicates when the strategy is invested in the dynamic VIX index, red when invested in the S&P 500. Source: Bloomberg.

If VIX > 15.6% for 27 consecutive days (previously 17.4% for 6 days)

> **Buy** your S&P dynamic VIX index[a]
>
> **Sell** your S&P 500 shares ETP[b]

Otherwise

> **Buy** your S&P 500 shares ETP
>
> **Sell** your S&P dynamic VIX index

---
[a]Such as XVZ.
[b]Such as SPY.

The performance of Strategy 1 suffered in 2012 because it was still biased towards dynamic VIX by setting its VIX threshold extremely low at 12.7%. By 2013 the strategy learned that stocks could rally and raised its VIX threshold and reaped the 19% S&P 500 rally that year. This was fortunate because dynamic VIX lost 18.1% in 2013. Strategy 1 can be thought of as a "best-of volatility or stocks" strategy. During sustained stock rallies (when VIX is below 16% for about a month) the strategy switches into stocks, but at the first sign of VIX rising the strategy switches into volatility.

Strategy 2 which switches between being long or short the short-term VIX futures indices was less affected by editing out the 20 most volatile days (see Figure 5.4). The window remained at one day because the short-term futures index demands quick reactions due to the high carry cost of being long. The threshold for going long increased slightly from 24.8% to 26.9%. The strategy made less profit overall but still performed extremely well with extremely high volatility.

If VIX closed above 26.9% (previously 24.8%) on the last trading day

    Buy your **long** S&P short-term VIX futures ETP[a]

    Sell your short S&P short-term VIX futures ETP[b]

otherwise if VIX closed below 24.8% on the last trading day

    Buy your **short** S&P short-term VIX futures ETP

    Sell your long S&P short-term VIX futures ETP

---
[a]Such as VXX.
[b]Such as SVXY.

If we now re-visit our optimal portfolio allocation the portfolio is completely transformed by removing the 20 most volatile days. Instead of a dynamic VIX allocation of over 30% we now find that just 11% allocation to dynamic VIX was best. Most of the diversification now comes from owning bonds; the allocation to the Barclays bond aggregate ETF (AGG) has increased from 31% to 48% and US Treasuries from 0% to 17%. So in summary, if we assume the immediate future will be unlikely to have catastrophic volatility events our allocation to dynamic VIX in a diversified portfolio should be much lower than recent history suggests. If you have $100 to invest then you would put $48 in the Barclays bond aggregate (AGG), $19 in the S&P 500 (SPY), $17 in US Treasury ETFs, $11 in a dynamic VIX ETN and just $5 in gold (GLD). Of course this is just a very rough guide. If you are worried about upcoming events you can sell some equity and move more money into your dynamic VIX ETN. Alternatively if you think that there are few risks ahead and equity will rally then you can cut your dynamic VIX allocation and move more money into equity.

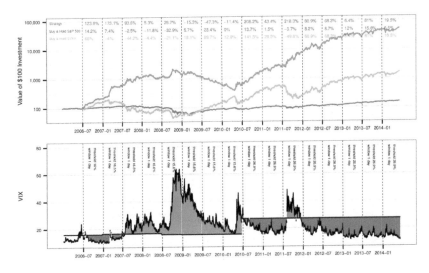

Figure 5.4: Long/short short-term VIX. Red shading indicates strategy is long volatility, blue indicates short volatility. Source: Bloomberg.

Future tail risks

In Chapter 2 we looked back over sixty years to see which events generated a rise in volatility. The past can be a good guide but new risks emerge all the time. If you want to keep abreast of the current risks then a good source of information is the World Economic Forum's Global Risks publication. This is freely available online[1] and is updated each year. The core of the publication is a survey of organizations associated with WEF and so, like any survey, is biased. But it does provide a clear and up-to-date list of global risks ranked according to a combination of the likelihood that the risk will materialize and the severity of the risk. For example "weapons of mass destruction" are seen as low probability risks with a high severity whereas "mismanaged urbanization" is seen as high probability but low impact. The top risks are both probable and severe in impact, and the top ten risks for 2014 are:

1. **Fiscal crises in key economies**. When a government spends more than it earns in taxes it has to borrow money in the bond market to plug the gap. This is called a fiscal deficit, and is usually measured as a per-

---

[1]http://www.weforum.org/risks

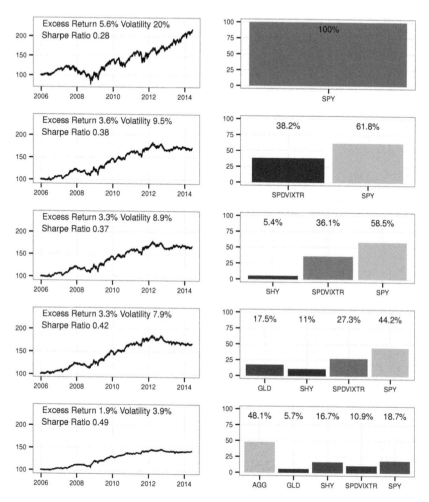

Figure 5.5: Graphs on left show return of $100 invested portfolios with the weights on the right. Returns and volatilities are annualized. Source: Bloomberg.

centage of GDP. If the fiscal deficit persists then there is the possibility the amount of debt will grow faster than GDP and spirals out of control leading to a sovereign bond default. Japan, the US and the UK all have large debt to GDP ratios and the report is citing this as its top risk in 2014.

2. **Structurally high unemployment/underemployment**. Following the Credit Crisis the number of unemployed people in the US and elsewhere rose sharply as companies reduced costs by firing staff. As people remain out of work for extended periods of time their skills become obsolete and they become less employable such that when the economy does recover they may be unable to work. Another source of structural unemployment is discrimination, because people who wish to work are not allowed to because of their gender, race, age or sexual orientation.

3. **Water crises**. One in six people on Earth, which is over one billion people, currently do not have access to clean drinking water. The most water-stressed regions, defined as having less than 1,700 cubic metres per person per year, are in China, India and Sub-Saharan Africa. Even in developed countries there are regions where population growth has exceeded the available water supply, for example in California in the United States. The fear is that water shortage will lead to political and even military conflict.

4. **Severe income disparity**. Income inequality is growing more extreme rather than reducing over time. An OECD study ("Divided We Stand: Why Inequality Keeps Rising", 2011) found that in the OECD countries the average income of the top 10% richest of the population is about nine times that of the poorest 10%. The ratio is higher in some countries: 10 to 1 in Italy, Japan, Korea and the UK, 14 to 1 in Israel, Turkey and the US, and 27 to 1 in Mexico and Chile. Globalization has been blamed as a driver of income inequality in emerging and developing countries.

5. **Failure of climate change mitigation**. The definitive report on climate change is produced by the Intergovernmental Panel on Climate Change (IPCC), which is the leading international body for the assessment of climate change. The report summary in 2007 is as follows: "Warming of the climate system is unequivocal, and since the 1950s, many of the observed changes are unprecedented over decades to millennia. The atmosphere and ocean have warmed , the amounts of snow and ice

have diminished, sea level has risen, and the concentrations of greenhouse gases have increased." The report also updates the forecast for the effects of climate change. Most importantly the contrast in precipitation between wet and dry regions and between wet and dry seasons will increase, so we can expect more extreme weather which may drive up commodity markets such as wheat and agricultural products. Also global mean sea level will continue to rise during the 21st century, which may lead to flooding of coastal cities, but this change will be slower and is unlikely to affect volatility in the short term.

6. **Greater incidence of extreme weather**. Climate change has been blamed for more frequent floods, storms and fires. This in turn creates development and security issues, such as food security and political and social instability.

7. **Global governance failure**. The reason why many of the risks have not been averted is due to a failure of governance. Therefore this risk is most connected to others. Global institutions are too ineffectual to compete with national and political interests, and this foils attempts to cooperate on addressing global risks.

8. **Food crises**. One of the top societal risks in the report, food crises occur when access to appropriate quantities and quality of food and nutrition becomes inadequate or unreliable. Food crises are strongly linked to the risk of climate change and related factors.

9. **Failure of major financial mechanism/institution**. After the collapse of Lehman Brothers confidence in banks was severely shaken. The global bank regulator the Basel Committee on Banking Supervision has therefore identified the largest and most interconnected banks which are labelled global systemically important financial institutions (G-SIFIs). G-SIFIs have to comply with very strict and conservative rules on the risks they take with their capital called Basel III. Regulators are notorious for regulating against the *previous* crisis but may not help protect against the next crisis which will likely be different in nature.

10. **Profound political and social instability**. At number 10 is the risk that one or more systemically critical countries will experience significant erosion of trust and mutual obligations between states and citizens. This could lead to state collapse, internal violence, regional or global instability and, potentially, military conflict.

Some of these have had a proven impact on volatility, in particular 1 (Credit Crisis, European sovereign debt crisis) and 9 (Lehman, Washington Mutual). Others, such as water crises, are unlikely to affect US volatility in the near term. So it is important to note that some issues which the WEF consider risky may not be relevant to you as a volatility investor. However the report is worth reading because it will give you a list of keywords to look out for as you read the news.

Another good source of information is the IMF Global Financial Stability Report. This is published twice a year in April and October and is quite lengthy and analytical and assumes some financial knowledge. However the GFSR is focussed on markets, and so is very relevant to volatility investors. The report is freely available and the IMF produces press conference videos summarizing key findings from the report. The first chapter summarizes the state of the global financial system using a set of stability indicators produced by the IMF, then it goes into the detail of the state of markets in each region. The rest of the report is more variable and depends on the particular problems of the moment. At the back there is a useful glossary in case you are not familiar with some of the financial terms.

Summary

Volatility is not trending higher The massive volatility event occurred during the Great Depression in the 1930s. The Credit Crisis is dwarfed by volatility during that period. Realized volatility since 1880 has averaged around 17% (dipping below during equity rallies and above during crises). There is little evidence that the "base" level of volatility is increasing.

Forgetting the Credit Crisis By snipping out the 20 most volatile days since 1990 (which all occurred in 2008) we can re-tune our trading strategies for a calmer decade ahead. For a portfolio this cuts the optimal allocation to dynamic VIX from 30% to 10%. The optimal risk-adjusted portfolio for the "edited" period from 2006 to 2014 would have, for every $100 invested: $48 in the Barclays bond aggregate (AGG), $19 in the S&P 500 (SPY), $17 in US Treasury ETFs (SHY), $11 in a dynamic VIX ETN (such as XVZ) and just $5 in gold (GLD).

Future tail risks There are two reports to read regularly to keep up to date with current crises. These are the World Economic Forum's annual

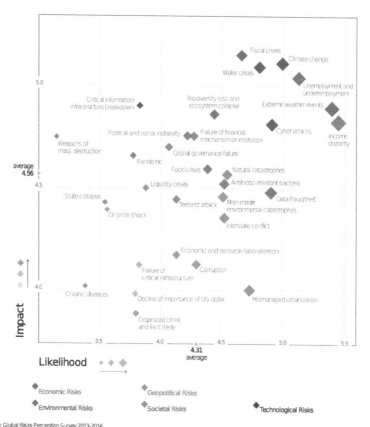

Source: Global Risks Perception Survey 2013-2014.
Note: Survey respondents were asked to assess the likelihood and impact of the individual risks on a scale of 1 to 7, 1 representing a risk that is not likely to happen or have impact, and 7 a risk very likely to occur and with massive and devastating impacts.

Figure 5.6: World Economic Forum top risks by likelihood and impact for 2014. Source: "Global Risks", World Economic Forum, Switzerland, 2014.

"Global Risks" publication and the IMF's "Global Financial Stability Report" published twice a year in April and October. These lists provide you, the volatility investor, with a set of current risks to help inform and time your trades.

Volatility Glossary

Tickers in [parentheses] show VIX ETPs that have been withdrawn.

[AAVX] UBS ETRACS Daily Short 1-Month S&P 500 VIX Futures ETN

[BBVX] UBS ETRACS Daily Short 2-Month S&P 500 VIX Futures ETN

[CCVX] UBS ETRACS Daily Short 3-Month S&P 500 VIX Futures ETN

CVOL *C-Tracks Citi Volatility Index Total Return ETN.* The C-Tracks Exchange-Traded Notes (the "C-Tracks") linked to the Citi Volatility Index Total Return (the "Index") provide investors with an investable means to gain directional exposure to the implied volatility of large-cap U.S. stocks. The Index methodology combines a daily rolling long exposure to the third- and fourth-month futures contracts on the CBOE Volatility Index (the "VIX Index") with a short exposure to the S&P 500 Total Return Index. The VIX futures contracts exposure is constantly maintained, but the weighting of the S&P 500 Total Return Index is variable and determined monthly via a backward-looking linear regression.

[DDVX] UBS ETRACS Daily Short 4-Month S&P 500 VIX Futures ETN

DLVO *Lyxor UCITS ETF Dynamic Long VIX Futures Index (EUR).* This is a UCITS IV compliant, open-ended Exchange Traded Fund incorporated in Luxembourg. The investment objective is to track both the upward and downward evolution of the Dynamic Long VIX Futures Index, representative of a strategy on the US equity market expected volatility through a basket of S&P 500 VIX futures listed on the CBOE.

DLVX *Lyxor UCITS ETF Dynamic Long VIX Futures Index.* This is a UCITS IV compliant, open-ended Exchange Traded Fund incorporated in Luxembourg. The investment objective is to track both the upward and downward evolution of the Dynamic Long VIX Futures Index, representative of a strategy on the US equity market expected volatility through a basket of S&P 500 VIX futures listed on the CBOE.

DSVO *Lyxor UCITS ETF Dynamic Short VIX Futures Index (EUR).* This is a UCITS IV compliant, open-ended Exchange Traded Fund incorporated in Luxembourg. The investment objective is to track both the upward and downward evolution of the Dynamic Short VIX Futures Index, representative of a strategy on the US equity market expected volatility through a basket of S&P 500 VIX futures listed on the CBOE.

DSVX *Lyxor UCITS ETF Dynamic Short VIX Futures Index.* This is a UCITS IV compliant, open-ended Exchange Traded Fund incorporated in Luxembourg. The investment objective is to track both the upward and downward evolution of the Dynamic Short VIX Futures Index, representative of a strategy on the US equity market expected volatility through a basket of S&P 500 VIX futures listed on the CBOE.

[EEVX] UBS ETRACS Daily Short 5-Month S&P 500 VIX Futures ETN

[FFVX] UBS ETRACS Daily Short 6-Month S&P 500 VIX Futures ETN

[IVO] iPath Inverse January 2021 S&P 500 VIX Short-Term Futures ETN

IVOP *iPath Inverse S&P 500 VIX Short-Term Futures ETN II.* Designed to provide investors with inverse exposure to the S&P 500 VIX Short-Term Futures Index Excess Return. The S&P 500 VIX Short-Term Futures Index Excess Return is designed to reflect the returns that are potentially available through an unleveraged investment in short-term futures contracts on the CBOE Volatility Index. The Index offers exposure to a daily rolling long position in the first and second month VIX Index futures contracts and reflects the implied volatility of the S&P 500 at various points along the volatility forward curve.

LVX *Lyxor ETF S&P 500 VIX Futures Enhanced Roll.* This is a UCITS IV compliant, open-ended Exchange Traded Fund incorporated in Luxembourg. The investment objective is to track both the upward and downward evolution of the S&P 500 VIX Futures Enhanced Roll Index (SPVIXETR) representative of a strategy on the US equity market expected volatility through a basket of S&P 500 VIX futures.

LVO *Lyxor ETF S&P 500 VIX Futures Enhanced Roll (EUR).* This is a UCITS IV compliant, open-ended Exchange Traded Fund incorporated in Luxembourg. The investment objective is to track both the upward and downward evolution of the S&P 500 VIX Futures Enhanced Roll Index (SPVIXETR) representative of a strategy on the US equity market expected volatility through a basket of S&P 500 VIX futures.

MHDU *JP Morgan/Source Macro Hedge Dual ETF (EUR).* This ETF is a UCITS III compliant exchange-traded investment fund incorporated in Ireland. The objective of the fund is to track the performance of the J.P. Morgan Macrohedge Dual Total Return Index.

MHUU *JP Morgan/Source Macro Hedge US ETF.* This ETF is a UCITS III compliant exchange-traded investment fund incorporated in Ireland. The objective of the Fund is to track the performance of the J.P. Morgan Macrohedge US Total Return Index.

SVXY *ProShares Short VIX Short-Term Futures ETF.* This ETF seeks daily investment results, before fees and expenses, that correspond to the inverse (-1x) of the daily performance of the S&P 500 VIX Short-Term Futures Index.

TVIX *VelocityShares Daily 2x VIX Short-Term ETN.* The return on these ETNs is linked to twice (2x) the daily performance of the S&P 500 VIX Short-Term Futures Index ER less the investor fee.

TVIZ *VelocityShares Daily 2x VIX Medium-Term ETN.* The return on the ETNs is linked to twice (2x) the daily p erformance of the S&P 500 VIX Mi d-Term Futures Index ER less the investor fee.

ULVO *Lyxor ETF Unleveraged S&P 500 VIX Futures Enhanced Roll (EUR).* This ETF aims to obtain a variable (up to 50% exposure) to increases or decreases in the volatility of the S&P 500 index, by partially tracking the S&P 500 Vix Futures Enhanced Roll Index, while using money-market instruments to limit value-at-risk.

ULVX *Lyxor ETF Unleveraged S&P 500 VIX Futures Enhanced Roll.* This ETF aims to obtain a variable (up to 50% exposure) to increases or decreases in the volatility of the S&P 500 index, by partially tracking the S&P 500 Vix Futures Enhanced Roll Index, while using money-market instruments to limit value-at-risk

UVXY *ProShares Ultra VIX Short-Term Futures ETF.* This ETF seeks daily investment results, before fees and expenses, that correspond to two times (2x) the daily performance of the S&P 500 VIX Short-Term Futures Index.

VIIX *VelocityShares VIX Short-Term ETN.* The return on the ETNs is linked to the daily performance of the S&P 500 VIX Short-Term Futures Index ER less the investor fee.

VIIZ *VelocityShares VIX Medium-Term ETN.* The return on the ETNs is linked to the daily performance of the S&P 500 VIX Mid-Term Futures Index ER less the investor fee.

VIXH *First Trust CBOE S&P 500 VIX Tail Hedge Fund ETF.* The Fund seeks investment results that correspond generally to the price and yield, before the Fund's fees and expenses, of an equity index called the CBOE VIX Tail Hedge Index.

VIXM *ProShares VIX Mid-Term Futures ETF.* This ETF seeks investment results, before fees and expenses, that track the performance of the S&P 500 VIX Mid-Term Futures Index.

VIXS *Source S&P 500 VIX Short-Term Futures ETF.* This is a UCITS III compliant exchange traded investment fund incorporated in Ireland. The objective of the fund is to track the performance of the S&P 500 VIX Short-Term Futures Total Return Index.

VIXY *ProShares VIX Short-Term Futures ETF.* This ETF seeks investment results, before fees and expenses, that track the performance of the S&P 500 VIX Short-Term Futures Index.

VOLT *Source/Nomura Voltage Mid-Term ETF.* This UCITS ETF aims to provide the performance of the Nomura Voltage Strategy Mid-Term 30-day USD Total Return Index. The Index aims to capture spikes in volatility, while mitigating the cost of holding a long-volatility position through VIX futures.

VSXX *iPath VSTOXX Short-Term Futures ETN.* This ETN is issued by Barclays Bank PLC in Germany. The Note will provide investors with a cash payment at the scheduled maturity or early redemption, based on the performance of the underlying index, the EURO STOXX 50 Volatility Short-Term Futures Total Return Index.

VSXY *iPath VSTOXX Mid-Term Futures ETN*. This ETN is issued by Barclays Bank PLC in Germany. The Note will provide investors with a cash payment at the scheduled maturity or early redemption, based on the performance of the underlying index, the EURO STOXX 50 Volatility Mid-Term Futures Total Return Index.

[VXAA] UBS ETRACS 1-Month S&P 500 VIX Futures ETN

[VXBB] UBS ETRACS 2-Month S&P 500 VIX Futures ETN

[VXCC] UBS ETRACS 3-Month S&P 500 VIX Futures ETN

[VXDD] UBS ETRACS 4-Month S&P 500 VIX Futures ETN

[VXEE] UBS ETRACS 5-Month S&P 500 VIX Futures ETN

[VXFF] UBS ETRACS 6-Month S&P 500 VIX Futures ETN

VXIM *iPath S&P 500 VIX Mid-Term Futures ETN*. This ETN is issued in Germany. The Note will provide investors with a cash payment at the scheduled maturity or early redemption based on the performance of the underlying index, the S&P 500 Mid-Term VIX Futures Total Return Index.

VXIS *iPath S&P 500 VIX Short-Term Futures ETN*. This ETN is issued in Germany. The Note will provide investors with a cash payment at the scheduled maturity or early redemption based on the performance of the underlying index, the S&P 500 Short-Term VIX Futures Total Return Index.

VXX *iPath S&P 500 VIX Short-Term Futures ETN*. Designed to provide investors with exposure to the S&P 500 VIX Short-Term Futures Index Total Return. The S&P 500 VIX Short-Term Futures Index Total Return is designed to provide access to equity market volatility through CBOE Volatility Index futures. The Index offers exposure to a daily rolling long position in the first and second month VIX futures contracts and reflects the implied volatility of the S&P 500 at various points along the volatility forward curve.

VXZ *iPath S&P 500 VIX Mid-Term Futures ETN*. This ETN will provide investors with a cash payment at the scheduled maturity or early redemption based on the performance of its underlying index, the S&P 500 Mid-Term VIX Futures Total Return Index.

[VZZ] iPath Long Enhanced S&P 500 VIX Mid-Term Futures ETN

[VZZB] iPath Long Enhanced S&P 500 VIX Mid-Term Futures ETN II

XIV *VelocityShares Daily Inverse VIX Short-Term ETN.* The return on the ETNs is linked to the inverse of the daily performance of the S&P 500 VIX Short-Term Futures Index ER less the investor fee.

XVIX *UBS E-TRACS Daily Long-Short VIX ETN.* This ETN will provide investors with a cash payment at the scheduled maturity or early redemption based on the performance of the underlying index, the S&P 500 Index VIX Term-Structure Excess Return. This index is a composite index that measures the return from taking a long 100% position in the S&P 500 VIX Mid-Term Futures Index Excess Return with a short, or inverse, 50% position in the S&P 500 VIX Short-Term Futures Index Excess Return with daily rebalancing of the long and short positions.

XVZ *iPath S&P 500 Dynamic VIX ETN.* This ETN will provide investors with a cash payment at the scheduled maturity or early redemption based on the performance of its underlying index, the S&P 500 Dynamic VIX Futures Total Return Index.

XXV *iPath Inverse S&P 500 VIX Short-Term Futures ETN.* Designed to provide investors with inverse exposure to the S&P 500 VIX Short-Term Futures Index Excess Return. The S&P 500 VIX Short-Term Futures Index Excess Return is designed to reflect the returns that are potentially available through an unleveraged investment in short-term futures contracts on the CBOE Volatility Index. The Index offers exposure to a daily rolling long position in the first and second month VIX Index futures contracts and reflects the implied volatility of the S&P 500 at various points along the volatility forward curve.

ZIV *VelocityShares Daily Inverse VIX Medium-Term ETN.* The return on the ETNs is linked to the inverse of the daily performance of the S&P 500 VIX Mid-Term Futures Index ER less the investor fee.

Look at issuer sites for the latest products, and to get a detailed prospectus for each product listed above:

iPath http://www.ipathetn.com/us

E-TRACS http://www.ibb.ubs.com/mc/etracs_US

ProShares http://www.proshares.com

Source http://www.source.info

VelocityShares http://www.velocityshares.com

C-Tracks http://www.c-tracksetns.com

These are volatility indices for various global equity markets. Indices which start with the letter "V", such as VIX and VSTOXX, are the percentage volatility to be expected for the following 30 days for options on shares in their respective stock index and are generally uninvestible. Indices which start with "S" such as SPDVIXTR are total return indices created by Standard and Poor's which are based on positions in VIX futures and are tracked by several ETPs.

SPDVIXTR *S&P 500 Dynamic VIX Futures Index* dynamically allocates between the S&P 500 Short-Term VIX Futures and S&P 500 Mid-Term VIX Futures Indices by monitoring the steepness of the implied volatility curve and to provide a cost-efficient exposure to forward implied volatility.

SPVIXETR *S&P 500 VIX Futures Enhanced Roll* dynamically switches between a short-term VIX futures portfolio and a mid-term VIX futures portfolio in order to model cost efficient exposure to volatility in the broad equity market.

SPVIXSTR *S&P 500 VIX Short-Term Futures Index* utilizes prices of the next two near-term VIX futures contracts to replicate a position that rolls the nearest month VIX futures to the next month on a daily basis in equal fractional amounts. This results in a constant one-month rolling long position in first and second month VIX futures contracts.

SPVIXMTR *S&P 500 VIX Mid-Term Futures Index* measures the return of a daily rolling long position in the fourth, fifth, sixth and seventh month VIX futures contracts.

VDAX *VDAX-NEW Index.* Measures volatility of the DAX index of the 30 most actively traded German stocks traded on the Frankfurt stock exchange.

VHSI *HSI Volatility Index.* Measures volatility of the Hang Seng index which includes the largest and most liquid stocks listed on the Main Board of the Stock Exchange of Hong Kong.

VIX *Chicago Board Options Exchange (CBOE) Volatility Index.* Measures volatility of the S&P 500 index which includes 500 leading companies in leading industries of the U.S. economy, giving 75% coverage of U.S. equities.

VNKY *Nikkei Stock Average Volatility Index.* Measures volatility of the Nikkei 225 which is a price-weighted equity index consisting of 225 stocks in the first section of the Tokyo Stock Exchange.

VSMI *Volatility Index on the SMI.* Measures volatility of the SMI index, which comprises 20 of the largest and most liquid stocks in the Swiss equity market.

VSTOXX *EURO STOXX 50 Volatility Index.* Measures volatility of the EURO STOXX 50 Index of supersector leaders in the Eurozone. EURO STOXX covers 50 stocks from 12 Eurozone countries: Austria, Belgium, Finland, France, Germany, Greece, Ireland, Italy, Luxembourg, the Netherlands, Portugal and Spain.

VXD *Chicago Board Options Exchange Dow Jones Industrial Average Volatility Index.* Measures the volatility of the Dow Jones Industrial Average which is a price-weighted measure of 30 leading U.S. companies.

VXN *Chicago Board Options Exchange NASDAQ-100 Volatility Index.* The NASDAQ-100 includes 100 of the largest US domestic and international non-financial securities listed on The Nasdaq Stock Market based on market capitalization. The Index reflects companies across major industry groups including computer hardware and software, telecommunications, retail/wholesale trade and biotechnology.

VXV *Chicago Board Options Exchange S&P 500 3-Month Volatility Index* Designed to be a constant measure of 3-month implied volatility of the S&P 500 Index options. The VXV Index has tended to be less volatile than the CBOE Volatility Index (VIX), which measures one-month implied volatility. Using the VXV and VIX indices together provides useful insight into the term structure of S&P 500 option implied volatility.

In addition to equity volatility indices, the Chicago Board Options Exchange produces volatility indices that track the volatility of exchange traded products. These offer a way to express a view on the volatility of emerging market equity (Brazil and China), currencies, and commodities like oil, gold and silver:

VXEWZ CBOE Brazil ETF Volatility Index, which reflects the implied volatility of the EWZ ETF.

VXGDX CBOE Gold Miners ETF Volatility Index (ticker VXGDX), which reflects the implied volatility of the GDX ETF.

VXFXI CBOE China ETF Volatility Index (ticker VXFXI), which reflects the implied volatility of the FXI ETF.

VXSLV CBOE Silver ETF Volatility Index (ticker VXSLV), which reflects the implied volatility of the SLV ETF.

VXEEM CBOE Emerging Markets ETF Volatility Index (ticker VXEEM), which reflects the implied volatility of the EEM ETF, the iShares MSCI Emerging Markets Index.

OVX CBOE Crude Oil ETF Volatility Index ("Oil VIX", Ticker OVX) measures the market's expectation of 30-day volatility of crude oil prices by applying the VIX methodology to United States Oil Fund, LP (Ticker - USO) options spanning a wide range of strike prices.

GVZ CBOE Crude Oil Volatility Index (OVX) based on United States Oil Fund option prices; and also the CBOE EuroCurrency Volatility Index (EVZ) based on CurrencyShares Euro Trust (FXE) options. GLD is an exchange traded fund (ETF) that represents fractional, undivided interest in the SPDR Gold Trust, which primarily holds gold bullion. As such, the performance of GLD is intended to reflect the spot price of gold, less fund expenses.

EVZ CBOE EuroCurrency Volatility Index ("Euro VIX", Ticker EVZ) measures the market's expectation of 30-day volatility of the EURUSD exchange rate by applying the VIX methodology to options on the CurrencyShares Euro Trust (Ticker FXE). FXE is an exchange traded fund that holds euro on-demand deposits in euro denominated bank accounts. As such, the performance of FXE is intended to reflect the EURUSD exchange rate, less fund expenses.

VXXLE CBOE Energy Sector ETF Volatility Index. Reflects the implied volatility of the XLE ETF.

For details on individual volatility indices which are tracked by the exchange traded products, please refer to the web sites of the index companies:

CBOE VIX Microsite http://www.cboe.com/micro/VIX

Deutsche http://www.dax-indices.com/EN

J.P.Morgan Tradable Indices http://www.jpmorganindices.com

Standard & Poor's Dow Jones Indices http://www.spindices.com

STOXX http://www.stoxx.com

Index

Lightning Source UK Ltd.
Milton Keynes UK
UKHW020607160622
404517UK00002B/13

9 780956 663511